The Bounce Back Journey of Careers

AN INSPIRING COLLECTION OF PERSONAL STORIES

Compiled by
Discover Your Bounce Publishing

DEDICATION

This book is dedicated to anyone on a career path. Through your highs and lows we hope you find within this book the inspiration and bravery to establish the career of your dreams.

CONTENTS

FOREWORD
By Sharon Critchlow

This book was compiled after 12 months of the Covid-19 pandemic, during a period of lockdown. The world of work has changed with more flexible and home-based working environments available than in the pre-Covid era. Workers have been experiencing isolation, difficulties with switching off from work, furlough, concerns about having a long term job and general mental strain. Research by TotalJobs indicated that 69 per cent of workers now want an enhanced focus on work/life balance as the world opens up. The impact for individuals and employers is set to continue and the world of work may never be the same again.

We have noticed that workers, both employed and self-employed, have had a period of reflection due to Covid. Questions have arisen in the quiet times, that would normally be dismissed when times are busy.

Do I really miss my job?

Would I prefer to be doing something else?

I consider this an excellent time to expand your horizons and take the plunge in to a new career or a new challenge. The good thing with Covid is that it can provide perfect and understandable reason for leaving one place and trying something new, even if you move on again soon afterwards. The world is in flux, everything is changing, so why not change with it? After all, you only have one life.

Fear of Change

Research conducted by the London Business School concluded that 47 per cent of the 1,000 individuals surveyed wanted a change in careers. These results were reflected in similar surveys carried out in 2020 and 2021 by the Telegraph and the Guardian. This research also revealed that while many people do not enjoy what they do, a lot of them are not willing to risk a career change. Fear for the future and 'better the devil you know' often leaves people waiting with a feeling of being uncomfortably comfortable for between one and two years before making the change.

With the world making a digital leap in to the future, inevitably even those who aren't looking to move roles may end up with no choice. Redundancy could lead to the opportunity to try something new, and there are examples in this book where people have done just that and wondered why they didn't move years before!

Financial security is a big pull for keeping people stuck in an unsuitable role, with around a third of people citing it as why they don't feel they can move. Uncertainty of finding something better is another reason, as is the sad fact that many people cannot imagine feeling happy while at work. Finding the thing that makes you, you, is vital not only to your own happiness, fulfilment and joy, but to the economy as well. With such a high proportion of people unhappy, is it any wonder the UK was 15.1 per cent less productive than the rest of the G7 in 2016? The old ways of working are clearly not producing the desired result for many people and seem to be more and more in conflict with how we wish to live our lives.

A Life in Balance

When you are doing the wrong job for you, you are not in flow. The job ceases to be an expression of your talents and your energy can be used up very quickly. This leads to burnout and a loss of your talent to the world. As a coach I often see people in this quandary and this book is aimed at providing some examples of how a positive step can be taken forward, even from a dark place.

Not all change comes as a desperate move; it should also be acknowledged that what suited you last year may not suit you now. We all change and grow and we are all influenced by every experience we have in life. As my coaching teacher once said, "All of life is coaching." So if you wake up one day and think, 'I know I'm good at this job but I'm bored, I'm frustrated, there must be more to life,'—well there is! Life is there to be joyously experienced, so what needs to change to light that flame in you? What do you dream about? What are you passionate about? What would you do if you knew you couldn't fail?

It Is Never Too Late…

In this book we have brought together people who have taken the leap and thrived. Losing businesses, selling businesses, redundancies, pregnancies and ill health have been the start of an exciting new chapter for many of these authors. We hope that you feel encouraged when you read their stories and that you take some time for yourself to understand, develop and share your uniqueness with the world. It is never too late to do something different.

"Success is not final; failure is not fatal: it is the courage to continue that counts."

Winston Churchill

ANDREA SEXTON

Andrea started her career after university as a professional horse rider and learned first-hand during this time how to do her own media relations and sponsorship management.

This knowledge led her into her first brand management and marketing role. Having run her own PR company, Admire PR, since 2005, Andrea is an advocate for education about PR and how it is relevant for all businesses and business people.

Follow these links to connect with Andrea:

https://www.linkedin.com/in/andrea-sexton-14a3361a/

https://www.facebook.com/AdmirePR

https://www.instagram.com/asextonpr

https://www.twitter.com/ASextonPR

Pony Lover to PR

"So, are you still playing with horses?"

That's what my family would ask me a lot of the time as I grew up. It's okay as a hobby when you're a kid and you are at Pony Club, but riding wasn't supposed to last. It's not supposed to be a career. Then everybody asks you, when are you going to start doing something serious?

The Quiet Kid

I wasn't a very confident child but being in the world of horses and riding, this was the thing that I knew I could do. I had an ability to communicate with the horses, to get along with those horses that other people didn't. And at the time it was the only thing I did where I really had a lot of confidence in myself. At school, the only lesson I was confident in was art. And I had a choice when I did my A levels whether I went to art school or whether I went to an agricultural college or to a vet school to study Equine Science. I chose the science route. I chose what felt right for me at the time. I ended up at Bristol University, which was a real privilege. It was basically like doing an exercise physiology and sports performance degree for horses.

I had a really good time and I grew much more confident in myself through academic work and being able to present my knowledge. It helped me start to become who I am today.

More Horses

I remember finishing my degree and I didn't really know what to do next. I didn't feel like I was ready to go into any kind of what would be called 'a traditional' line of work. I got offered a job as a Yard Manager for a lady I worked for through the university. I was earning very little, but I was good at it and it meant I rode a lot of different horses, went to a lot of the events and learned about dressage as a sport which was new for me. It was a great grounding for me in the equestrian industry.

I really enjoyed that job and then it got to the point where it was time for me to move on. I found a job working for an Olympic rider. She was an incredible woman, and I learned so much from her and so many things that I still use in business today. I learned the way she conducted herself and the way she did everything as an athlete.

She sadly passed away at a very young age, not long after the Beijing Olympics and I hope she knew what I thought of her and what she gave to me. I'd like to think that she would be proud of where I've got to now.

When you are working for those people, who really are near the top in the world at what they do, it's an incredible privilege. I feel really lucky that I had that opportunity. It was really hard. It scared me often, to live up to the standard required. I get told now that in business you need to get comfortable with being uncomfortable. I was often uncomfortable at that job, it really tested me as a person. I was still quite shy, quite timid and I didn't tell anyone that I try not to let that show. But I had an ability with the horses and because of that ability I had the confidence to go to work each day. It showed me what I was capable of doing and that I could go to a very uncomfortable place and stay in it.

New Horizons

It was time for me to find a new career. I took a job lecturing that also fitted in with my riding. I really enjoyed that role. I loved teaching, loved lecturing and loved supporting young people. So much so, that mentoring is something that I still do today in my business. It's really important to me that I mentor as many young people as I can, those that work for me and those who are looking to work in communications related jobs elsewhere. I really struggled with the red tape in the college environment. Perhaps I'm not very good at following rules!

So I started to look around for another job. And then, I was so lucky I saw a job advertised for my favourite equestrian clothing brand, it was the brand belonging to a lady who was my complete hero for many, many years.

Starting Out in Brands

Anky Van Grunsven is a multiple Olympic and World champion, and in 2005 was a hugely influential rider. She was one of the first riders to create her own clothing line and it was ground breaking. It was one of the first brilliant technical ranges of clothing for the equestrian world. It was an exciting time to be involved in a brand like that and I could see the potential.

I realised that what I learned, by going to the shows, being on the circuit and immersed in dressage for so long, had given me a good grounding in the industry. I felt very lucky to get the opportunity to apply and get that job and travelled to the Netherlands to meet Anky and the ATC team. I hadn't really travelled on my own much before and this was the start of me learning that I love travelling and love speaking to and meeting new people. I also discovered that brand management, branding, developing something that the consumer really wants and desires, and all the different ways to market and promote that product, was something that excited me. I wanted to learn more.

In those first few days when I was out selling the clothing line I was scared! I had done a few sales roles but really nothing on this scale. I managed to sell some pieces and luckily the first collection I was involved with selling had a popular name and people wanted to buy it. The fact that I was new at selling and was learning on the job wasn't too much of a disadvantage.

I found the wider part of marketing easier; the organising of trade stands and making partnerships with riders and retailers.

The General Manager from ATC, Monique Van Dooren, moved on to a new role with a German equestrian company. She was my mentor and I didn't feel like I could stay at ATC without her. I was still learning the job and felt like I needed her leadership and knowledge to help me.

I was lucky enough to have the opportunity to carry on working with her at her new company where I could basically do the same job. The first day I met her when we talked about the new role I was pregnant. It was December 2007 at Olympia International Horse Show and I drove there and back in the day because I was quite heavily pregnant.

I'm so fortunate that me being pregnant wasn't really thought of as being a problem. I knew I wanted to keep doing some part-time work as I'd seen friends have babies who had lost their careers and then were left struggling to return to work. I wanted to be able to keep my hand in.

Babies and Olympics

Jacob was born a little earlier than I anticipated in February 2008. After an initial break I managed to carry on working a bit from home and then Jake started to travel with me. We went to some shows and visited some of the retailers and Jake did some trade shows as a baby. He worked at Olympia the following year with me as a nine month old. And yeah, it was fun, I was learning the ropes. It was hard work with a baby but I enjoyed it.

Then I was blessed with baby number two in 2011, Daisy. I fully admit that I was worried now, not sure how I would cope with the two of them.

I took a pause for a bit, and decided what I wanted to do was focus more on the PR side of the work so that I could stay at home more. That decision coincided with a rider on the GBR equestrian team who was going to the London Olympics asking me to help her sort out her media relations and social media ahead of the games. This was a rider I had worked with through her sponsorship since 2008. She went on to win two medals at London, an incredible experience.

Then gradually some other work started to come in, while I was still working for the German company with Monique. At that time I also decided I wanted to learn more about the industry, and I found a Masters that I could do remotely. I studied Strategic Marketing and Luxury Brand Management at London Metropolitan University. It fitted really well with what I was doing with my work and the knowledge I needed to have. I started that Masters in 2013 and worked at it part-time over the next two years. I gradually continued building clients but always working part-time because of the children. In November 2014, I had my third child, Tom. It was quite a difficult pregnancy and it wasn't an easy birth so I feel enormously blessed he is in our lives. It might sound strange but my work did help to give me some self-confidence at that time. I continued to work part-time until 2019, when I started to work full-time and established my company Admire PR.

Admire PR

So things built up nicely over 2019 then we hit the pandemic last year. It's been a brutal year for many but I'm grateful that it gave me a chance to step back and look at how Admire can develop into the business I have always dreamed of.

The future's looking good. I've got a very clear vision for the business, who we work with and how we work. The vision encompasses everything I've learned on my journey so far. The time working with young people as a mentor and a support, the PR expertise I've learned from not only doing my own media and sponsorship, but with all the other clients over the past 15 years. All those things I learned through competing in sport as well as watching others at the top of their game. The tenacity required. The focus. The pure love of getting up every day to do something you believe in and adore.

All these things I learned through sport have really led me to this point now. The business is growing, we are taking on more staff, mainly young people who are looking for mentorship and career guidance, training young people who are brilliant writers who have curious minds. And also parents or carers who have some previous PR experience and who need some flexible work. The future's bright, and watch this space.

My top tips for curating your dream career:

- Follow your heart, what brings you joy?
- Read, be curious, and keep learning.
- Be careful whose advice you listen to. No one else can possibly know you like you do. Find a mentor or mentors who support you and will help you decide what's next at each stage.

"Business opportunities are like buses,
there's always another one coming."

Richard Branson

BEATRICE MARTIN

Bea has had countless jobs, including senior management roles in the NHS and financial services, before setting up a complementary health centre, travelling around the world, working in off-grid communities, and doing a lot of temping.

Based in the south west of England, Bea now lives and works with her partner David as part of the duo Bards of Avalon. They've been working full-time as sound therapists since 2010, releasing their first album when they were both 50. Their mission is to use sound therapy to enhance clients' health and wellbeing so they live a more joyful, fulfilling life. Like wandering minstrels, they also love to guide others around sacred sites with storytelling and live musical accompaniment. They're currently writing a book about their adventures.

You can find out more about Bea and the Bards of Avalon on:

https://www.bardsofavalon.com/

One in Ten

My humiliation was complete. I had a single pair of shoes and one of the heels had decided to snap in half. It was whilst I was in the dole queue, waiting to sign on. As I hobbled lopsidedly into the DHSS building, I asked myself, "Do I buy a new pair of shoes and have no money to eat, or do I walk around in wellies until I can afford shoes?"

It was 1982, I'd recently graduated from Sheffield University and now found myself amongst the three million plus unemployed.

I had decided to go to University when I was five years old, a curious ambition as no one in my family had been. I dreamed of being an explorer, a teacher and a writer. My parents wanted me to be a lawyer. As a dutiful daughter, I studied law for a while, convincing myself that I would fight for the rights of the downtrodden and oppressed. The reality was ploughing through endless tomes of case law. I seemed to spend hours in the law library trying to memorise vast amounts of data which bypassed my brain. I found it hard work and exceptionally boring. No matter how hard I studied, I couldn't pass the exams.

I switched to a course on Ancient History and Classical Civilisation which to others seemed like career suicide. However, I had been obsessed with the ancient world since childhood. I reasoned that if I followed my passion for my first degree, I could always do vocational training afterwards. The course covered a great variety of topics such as art, architecture, archaeology, language, literature, economics, philosophy, politics, sociology and history. I was very blessed to have lecturers who encouraged students to think for themselves. It was intellectually stimulating, fed my soul and brought me great joy.

During my final year, I experienced a debilitating digestive illness which left me exhausted. For the first couple of months after graduating I took the opportunity to rest and recharge. When September came, I was ready to apply for a job.

The goal of getting to university had been all-consuming. However, the problem was I hadn't really thought through what to do once I'd graduated. What was the point of studying if all I got was a piece of paper with letters at the end of my name and no job?

At the time, job vacancies were advertised in the weekly jobs section of the local newspaper or in the Jobcentre. The internet and mobile phones had yet to be invented. I didn't even have a landline telephone! If I needed to contact a potential employer, I had to use a payphone, write a letter or knock on a door.

These were the days long before personal computers became popular. Whilst handwritten CVs and application forms were acceptable, if I wanted to stand out amidst hundreds of other applicants, I needed a typewritten CV and found a professional typist to do this for me.

To boost my job prospects, I started driving lessons. I wasn't a confident driver and to my utter astonishment, passed the driving test first time. I also enrolled in an evening secretarial course learning touch typing and shorthand.

It became a full-time job looking for a full-time job. I was in a catch-22 situation: I couldn't get a job without experience and couldn't get experience without a job.

Norman Tebbit, the Secretary of State for Employment, had said the year before that, "I grew up in the '30s with an unemployed father. He didn't riot. He got on his bike and looked for work, and he kept looking till he found it." Well, I had taken personal responsibility, learned new skills and did everything I could to find a job and wasn't getting anywhere. The band UB40 spoke for me and many others when they sang, "I am the one in ten… a statistic, a reminder of a world that doesn't care."

I didn't want to leave Sheffield; it was my home. I'd met my fiancé and had all our friends there. Unfortunately, Sheffield's unemployment rate was well above the national average with the collapse of the steel and mining industries.

As the months rolled on, despair set in. I felt demoralised and a complete failure. In a school which was renowned for its academic excellence, we were threatened with, "You'll end up working in Woolworths" if we weren't diligent with our studies. Now, I couldn't even get a job in Woolworths. I learned very quickly that unemployment brought stigma and judgement. I just wanted to do something, anything, and feel useful.

I had an interview with the Jobcentre to review my job search. I dreaded those sessions as it was more about proving everything I'd done to try and get a job which only compounded my feelings of failure. However, this time was different. The adviser said to me that as I'd been unemployed for six months, I was now eligible for a new government sponsored Community Enterprise Programme run by the Manpower Services Commission.

The purpose of this programme was to provide training and job experience opportunities. With the demise of traditional industries, there was a need for people of all ages to acquire new skills and knowledge. The jobs were six months' long, many of which were part-time and could be done alongside day release courses at local colleges. The Jobcentre adviser handed me a card, saying that there was a vacancy for a full-time personal assistant, ideally a graduate, to assist with the formation of a community enterprise programme. To do the job I needed typing, shorthand and a driving licence. "I think this could be right up your street," the adviser said and without a second's hesitation I asked to be put forward for interview.

The scheme I applied for was in one of the most economically and socially deprived areas in Sheffield, deeply impacted by the decline in the steel industry. The plan was a simple yet ambitious one devised by a group of visionary Methodist ministers. They took their pastoral roles seriously and wanted to support the local community during harsh economic times. They had seven different church sites which, although busy on Sundays, lay empty the rest of the week. The ministers came up with a proposed scheme that would provide social projects such as lunch clubs for the elderly, a parents and toddlers group and a club for teenagers. There were plans for gardening and building maintenance teams to tend to the grounds and building repairs. The ministers were keen that youngsters with learning difficulties and ex-offenders also had these opportunities and so liaised with Mencap and Nacro to take placements.

I was very nervous when I was called to interview. I didn't have much self-esteem, and unemployment only served to knock my confidence. However, when Ian, one of the ministers, interviewed me and described his vision with evangelical passion, I thought my heart would burst for joy. I longed to be part of something that would make a difference and my enthusiasm shone through. I got the job!

I was one of the first to join the scheme. It was exciting to be at the start of creating an organisation, particularly one which was a social passion project. Our main focus was to recruit people for the teams. Everyone shared a common bond: we had all been unemployed, whether it was six months or considerably longer.

One of my jobs was to travel around the sites with the Finance Manager and give people their wages in little brown paper packets. So, I got to know everyone on the scheme, around 100 people. I'll never forget the day I spoke with one of our minibus drivers. He had worked for the steel industry for over 30 years. He had been a very specialist craftsman creating exquisite hand-crafted cutlery. As I handed his wages to him one day, he told me how he felt he had lost his pride as a man by being unemployed for over five years. He explained he was part of the generation where a man would come home on a Friday afternoon, hand his wages to the wife, and feel that he had done his job as a provider. He felt embarrassed that his wife had become the breadwinner. Now, he was driving elderly residents from their homes to the lunch club. He enjoyed the banter with his passengers, witnessing how they transformed when they chatted, ate and sang together. With tears in his eyes, he told me the pride he felt from impacting on others' lives in such a direct way was a feeling he'd never experienced. He told me that his next job would be supporting the community. I was delighted when he found a permanent job as a minibus driver for social services.

The scheme was so successful in helping team members get permanent jobs and further training that the ministers decided to apply for Community Programme Agency status. This meant increasing the scheme to 150 members. I had been with the scheme right from the start and made a proposal of how to take things forward. My ideas were well received, I was designated a key worker and given the role of Administration and Welfare Rights Manager. I supervised a team of nine secretarial and admin staff, co-ordinated a Life and Social Skills training programme for the 18- to 25-year-old group and provided welfare rights guidance.

Although I devoted many hours to this job, it never felt like hard work, more like creative play. I had been extremely fortunate to have my contract extended as a key worker but it was time for me to go. It was a great wrench to leave, however the skills and experience I had acquired enabled me to get a full-time permanent job in a personnel department supporting NHS Mental Health Services. Looking back, it seemed like an eternity looking for a job, yet in truth was just a tiny fragment of my life. It still remains one of the best jobs I ever did, because I know I made a difference. The most valuable lesson I gained from this experience was in the words of Gandhi, "The best way to find yourself is to lose yourself in the *service* of others."

"Every problem is a gift—without problems we would not grow."

Anthony Robbins

DAVID JOHNSON

David has worked in the private sector and civil service for over 30 years until, sparked by his father's sight loss, he became interested in alternative health therapies. This took him on an amazing journey where, by setting clear intentions and following intuition and synchronicities, transformed his life and the lives of others.

He now lives and works with his partner, Bea, as part of the duo Bards of Avalon. Their main focus is sound baths for groups or individuals, offering talks and presentations on the power of sound therapy and conducting well-being at work sessions. Their mission is to use sound therapy to enhance clients' health and wellbeing so they live a more joyful, fulfilling life. Like wandering minstrels, they also love to guide others around sacred sites with storytelling and live musical accompaniment. Much of their work is now online and the therapeutic effects have been acknowledged by hundreds of testimonials. David has a passion for photography which captures the essence of their experiences, acting as a chronicle of extraordinary synchronicities. They're currently writing a book based on their adventures.

Find out more about Bards of Avalon at:

https://www.bardsofavalon.com

Life Begins at 50

I was sitting in a government office with 40 staff one day sorting through my paperwork with Heather and Sarah sat nearby when Sarah turned to me saying, "You've been doing the same grade job now for a long time, why don't you put in for a promotion?" The answer I gave, I don't know where it came from, was, "I will be made redundant from this job and then I will do what I came here to do." The reaction I got from both ladies was very strong, especially Heather who said she had been hoping to take redundancy for many years and it's never happened.

Several months later there were rumours going around about the security of my post, eventually a meeting was called in Birmingham on 16 July 2008. People came from all over the country, with around 100 people present. The management team explained that much of our work would be outsourced to make cost savings and they would be making our posts redundant. They handed out envelopes to everyone present. I was told I was the only person who had two options, because of the timing and all of the delays I had become eligible for either redundancy or early retirement. I was the only person from my office in Bristol affected and it felt like the finger of fate was pointed at me. When I looked into the offer I was given, I realised I could retire on a small pension on my 50th birthday which fell only 17 days before the final deadline for all the staff to leave. As I am writing this story I thought I would check on the government changes with regard to early retirement and found that this practice of offering a pension to staff from the age of 50 was abolished only 11 months after I left.

Only three days later my partner, Bea, and I visited a big event at Earls Court, London called One Life Live which was aimed at enriching people's lives, to give people new ideas around work and careers through seminars, workshops, travel ideas, etc. We listened to an inspirational talk by David Hamilton on his book 'It's The Thought That Counts: Why Mind Over Matter Really Works' which reminds us that we create our own reality. Later, as I walked around some of the exhibition stands I noticed a large clear Perspex bowl around one metre across filled with hundreds of Oracle cards from Hay House. I was about to embark on a sacred journey to Guatemala and knew that on my return I had no idea what I would be doing. So I asked in my mind for some guidance and pulled the card entitled 'The Bard' from The Wisdom of Avalon Pack by Collett Baron–Reid. It showed an image of a wandering minstrel and had the words 'music, poetry, myth, history, the enchantment of storytelling'. As I looked at the image and read those words, I was convinced that this represented me. I turned to Bea and excitedly asked her to take my picture holding the card. As she did this, one of the staff rushed over and asked what we were doing and I was very animated in my explanation of the significance of this card. She said, "Well why don't you take it with you." So I smiled, thanked her and place the card carefully into my pocket.

On our first full day in Guatemala we were invited to sit in a large hall in a circle with the international group we had joined for our journey to the temples of the Maya. We were all asked to introduce ourselves to the group and as it came round to my turn I felt in my pocket, found the Bard card from Earls Court and without thinking stood up, gesturing towards Bea saying we are the Bards of Avalon from the south west of England and sat back down with no idea what had made me say that. After we had all introduced ourselves we were addressed by Don Alejandro Cirilo Perez Oxlaj, President of the National Council of Elders and a member of the Cabinet of Guatemala. He said he knew our group's leader Aluna Joy Yaxk'in and felt it important to speak to us as we set off on our journey through the Maya lands and so would be late for a meeting with the president and the rest of the cabinet.

On our return from this very special journey through Guatemala and Honduras, I signed on at the local Jobcentre having no real idea of what I wanted to do next. I felt one simple and easy possibility would be as a driver. The world had just gone through the financial crash of 2008 and the odds of finding a job were becoming slim, with the unemployment rate over seven percent and rising all the time. But the following week, Bea came home from work holding Wednesday's Evening Post, our local paper, and said, "Your job is inside," as she handed it to me. I was not particularly interested and waited until Friday to check the paper when I came across, at the top of a page, an advert for drivers. I knew I had to ring the number. I was asked to come in that afternoon but as Bea had a half-day on Fridays and we wanted to go to visit Gloucester, I replied, "I can't make it today how about next week?" The lady said, "Yes, that's fine, come on Monday morning." This was to be my first interview for a job in many years, so as I talked to Dean, the company's branch manager, I felt both anxious and excited. He asked me to come back and meet the boss from head office the next day but I said, "I'm sorry that I can't because I've got a cataract operation at the local hospital tomorrow morning." He said in that case I could see him on Wednesday, to which I agreed. The day after my operation I met up with some of the applicants, completed a test and was offered the job part-time. I explained that the strength of my new lens had changed my eye prescription so I needed to let the eye settle down and be tested for new glasses before I could take up a driving job. I was surprised, bearing in mind the economic climate, that they agreed to this and a few weeks later I started work.

Bea and I had made a wish list of places we would love to visit around Christmas 2008 and the list was almost exclusively European. When Bea found out that one of our favourite inspirational speakers was going to be at a conference being held in Zürich entitled 'A New World, If You Can Take It' being held in July, we decided there and then to go and started to make plans. At the time Bea was a contractor in the IT industry and had just been given an award for outstanding service. One week later, Bea was informed that the management in charge of the European branch had decided to move her job to Bulgaria, terminating her contract. So we both decided as we were going to visit Zürich anyway why not just carry on and visit all the places on our wish list. I was only working part-time so was still visiting the local Jobcentre. I handed in my paperwork for signing off and wrote 'I am going abroad looking for ideas to become self-employed' which was a thing that I have never contemplated before in my life as I had always worked for an employer. Following the conference, we had an amazing time using rail passes to travel throughout Europe. In an astounding coincidence, we were able to spend time with Henry Lincoln, the author, television presenter, scriptwriter and actor who was co-author of 'The Templar's Secret Island', on Bornholm in the middle of the Baltic Sea. My interest in visiting the island stemmed from accidently recording a documentary on my VCR about Henry Lincoln, shown between Dan Brown's The Da Vinci Code and his Angels and Demons premier on 14 May 2009.

Just before leaving Zürich we received an email from the founders of the ecovillage Bhrugu Aranya in Poland saying that because of a death in the family, causing them to fly back to USA, our visit had been cancelled. We wondered what we would do with that time. We did not need to wait long as the next email we received was an invitation to a wedding, south of Oslo in Norway, of a lovely couple who had become great friends during our journey through Guatemala. We accepted, adjusted our plans and all had such a wonderful time. We made many return visits, spending many months first in the south and later at their wonderful new dream home with a lake in a pine forest two hours north of Oslo.

We received an email from the lady who ran the Guatemala tour asking for people to house-sit for her in America. We both felt this was a brilliant idea but in reality it would simply be too expensive to go to America just to house-sit. The following day I received a phone call from Carolan, who was one of the participants on the Guatemala journey. She said, "I don't know why but I had a strong feeling I need to ask you to house-sit my cat," and my immediate response was, "Who told you?" As we had only decided we'd like to do that the night before. We agreed the dates from 1st September to 21st November. After we had settled into her home and life in Twickenham near London, Bea received a phone call from a friend, Isobel, in Scotland. She said, "I have been doing evening classes in music recording and have a mobile recording studio with two microphones, my own record label and can get recordings mastered by my tutor". We immediately told her to come to London and as we talked, she booked her flight, which would mean leaving her husband and two children behind. Two days later we collected her from Luton airport and we started the adventure of recording an album the following day around the kitchen table. We had been asked by many people for years to record an album but as we had no idea what we would sing, we had no instruments and could not read music we were told by music studios it would not really be possible. Our sounds are intuitive, coming to us in the moment. We have sung in many special places around the world where the group we travelled with told us they experienced those special places on a whole other level.

I remember sitting in the lounge a couple of days later thinking this is not an album, it's not long enough, at that time it was only 15 minutes long, it should have been 40 minutes. By the end of her long weekend visit we all knew that more work needed to be done and we were invited to Scotland, recording first at Isobel's home, then at a log cabin by a stream in the woods and eventually recording with my nephew in Bristol. It all finally came together and the album, 'The Archangel Transmissions', was released in June 2010 and amazingly was 40 minutes long! When everything had been done we needed to have a band name to put on the album and after coming up with lists of all sorts of names it dawned on us we had been given the name three days after my early retirement at 50, Bards of Avalon. We became self-employed in 2010 with a focus on sound. Through many synchronicities we now run workshops, give talks around our travels and have run guided tours. Doing the ever-changing job we love, we have come to do just as I declared back in 2008.

As I reflect on the words from the Bard card which read, 'music, poetry, myth, history, the enchantment of storytelling' that I drew from the wisdom of Avalon pack at the start of my story, I am astounded by the synchronicity with the work we do with sound, our talks and presentations recounting events from our travels to historic and sacred sites around the world. From the day we met at a sound workshop at Stonehenge, the journey seemed to unfold before us and it really has been a leap of faith we both took after leaving the security of the nine to five. We have connected with thousands of people through our work inspiring more joyful, fulfilling lives and many have been inspired to take their own leap of faith. Even now as I write this story, before the current global circumstances we had believed our sound work could not be done online but synchronicity stepped in and now we can reach many more people around the world, so if you feel inspired why not take that leap of faith yourself.

"And the day came when the risk to remain tight in a bud was more painful than the risk it took to blossom."

Anaïs Nin

ELENI KIRBY

Eleni lives in the beautiful Cotswolds in England. She works in the family business Kiki Kirby Coaching as the Business Operations Manager and is a mum to daughter Sophie who she has raised alone. Her family has and will always be at the heart of whatever she does.

She has recently launched a Parenting and Lifestyle blog which focusses on trying to balance being a working mum along with having fun, living life to the full, always being grateful, looking after her family, loving herself more and teaching her daughter to do the same.

Find out more about Kiki Kirby Coaching at:

https://www.kikikirbycoaching.com

Join Eleni's well-being community at
http://www.kikikirbycoaching.co.uk/happy-healthy-wellbeing-community

You can also find Eleni blogging about her journey around Parenthood and Lifestyle at https://www.meandmylittlelady.com

Allow Those Setbacks to Be Your Biggest Comeback

Sometimes, along the journey of life, we are faced with detours or redirections. At that point in time we do not entirely know what life will look like or what the outcome will be. However, I believe things happen for a reason and we need to keep moving forward and trust the process.

If we were to meet and you did not know my career history you would probably not see me as the failure I once saw myself to be. As I reflected whilst writing this chapter around my career, it triggered a lot of different emotions and feelings. Mostly positive ones.

A Little About Me

I grew up in Zimbabwe, Africa, but the country was facing political trouble which compelled us to leave and so I moved to the UK in 2003 at the age of 15 with my family and two suitcases. I finished my education in the UK, squeezing both year 10 and 11 into one year alongside babysitting once per week for three lovely children. I also worked as a waitress at weekends and had the odd temp job in a recruitment company where my sister worked. I had a real passion to work and wanted to be successful.

I finished school and went on to do a hairdressing apprenticeship and qualified as a hairdresser working in a family-run business. After I completed my advanced level in hairdressing, I moved to a bigger salon which was also a family-run business. I was very successful in my hairdressing career and had a busy portfolio of clients. I loved my job and all the people I worked with.

The time came to pursue my dream of working on the cruise ships as a hairdresser, travelling the world. I did this for the length of one contract (approximately six and a half months) and whilst working at sea I met my daughter's father. Our relationship grew very serious during this time and I made the choice to terminate my contract 2½ months early. I returned to the UK and took one month off to settle and figure out what I was going to do next. Instinctively, I knew I wanted to go back to a salon, but I felt like I had failed as I had given up such a great opportunity in the past. I started working for a telecoms company in customer service and spent my free weekends between Greece and the ships to visit my daughter's father. Eleven months later he was called to do National Service (the Army). Our relationship had really grown and I left my job, moved to Greece and joined him. We rented a home together and continued our journey.

Whilst living in Greece, financially I did not have to work, however, I did not want to sit at home not doing anything. My passion for hair returned and I wanted to go back into a salon but it was a door that was not opening. Speaking very little Greek, I decided to look for jobs that I could do where English was spoken. I found a job working for a British travel company selling holidays for 10 months. My partner's National Service ended and he returned to the ships as an officer on board and we agreed we didn't want to be apart. I couldn't go back to hairdressing on board as I had terminated my contract so we both decided I wouldn't work. At the age of 23 my career had come to a sudden standstill through the choices and decisions I had made for which I later suffered the consequences.

We had some wonderful times sailing and I was very fortunate to be in a position that allowed me to travel the world and be a lady of leisure. We got engaged and planned to marry and start a family. However, my sister unfortunately fell ill. Losing our mum at such a young age and being a top performer in her recruitment job led to burnout. I returned to the UK to help my dad take care of her, he had moved in with her as she was unable to take care of herself. Both of our families were important to us and my partner and I were both respectful of this and supported each other the best we could.

As I was in the UK for a long period, I decided it was time to start working again, I needed a focus as my sister recovered and returned to the working world. I started temping within different admin and customer service roles which lead me to a six-month temporary contract working in HR for a higher education establishment where I thrived and I was very sad when my contract came to an end.

During this time our dream was to have a family, but I will be honest, I wasn't quite ready. I do not think you ever are! It was also time for me to return to living in Greece again. I felt I had not had the career or working life I wanted. I seemed to give up too easily and often put everyone else's needs and dreams before my own, I lacked self-worth.

We planned and agreed that if it was meant for us to have a family it would happen and it did, which caught us by surprise. Unfortunately, we miscarried at seven weeks. We both wanted this more than anything, so we continued to try and we found ourselves pregnant again four months later.

Nine Months Later...

We embraced the journey of parenthood and our beautiful daughter was born. Our lives were still based around the ships between Greece and the UK. With a newborn baby it made it difficult for us to settle into this lifestyle and unfortunately this put an immense amount of stress and pressure on our relationship. When our daughter was seven months old, he left us.

My daughter and I returned to the UK after being on the ships for two months with him. I had nothing, no job, no home, nothing, just my little baby girl. Whilst my ex helped financially with our daughter, because we were not married, I was not entitled to anything and it all became challenging in many ways. I had to somehow pick up the pieces of my career and be a single parent. He did visit our daughter here in the UK during his vacations and we visited Greece, however, it was very tough and times were very challenging. We tried to remain amicable and on good terms, for our daughter, but even to this day it has its challenges.

My family were a great support to both my little girl and I during this time which allowed me to not have to work for the first two years of my daughter's life, which I am so very grateful for. I used this time to enjoy motherhood, to enjoy my baby girl and make the most of watching her grow.

Regaining My Career

At 28 years old it was time to put myself back out there, get a job...and start my career again. Where do I begin? I felt like a complete failure, I felt like I had done so many jobs and even though they were all successful, my working life was one big mess. I felt like I had wasted my hairdressing qualifications. I lost so much confidence in myself and really did not know where to even begin, how was I going to put this into a CV and make it look good enough to get a job? It took many attempts, I felt so embarrassed by all the gaps and the different jobs I'd had. I would sit and journal as I had been going for counselling and coaching, and then a few weeks later tear the pages out of my journal to act like the bad stuff did not happen. I saw myself as such a failure. What was I going to tell my daughter one day? Would I ever be able to go back to the working world?

As time went on, I had discussed different jobs with my dad and sister as we were still living with them. I needed a job that fitted around my daughter and my family as they were looking after her whilst I worked. I decided to apply for a job in our local supermarket, this seemed the best way to get me back out into the working world. I remember going for the interview, it was one of the most daunting experiences, good news though, I got the job, this really gave me such a boost. I could finally see some light, but I had very bad anxiety in the first few weeks and I would physically feel sick when my alarm used to go off to wake me up. Often, I would find myself hiding down the aisles when I would see someone I knew. Having to wake up at 4.30am and work until lunchtime and then coming home to my little girl, who was still a toddler, was challenging in many ways. All I could see was this failure. So many of my friends around me had very successful careers and families. I tried to pick up the hairdressing again on the side, but I just didn't have the confidence anymore.

Amid the chaos of living under one roof with my dad and my sister, my sister was also setting up her own coaching business, in her bedroom. It was madness! But somehow, we pulled together and made it work as we all had each other. One year passed and things started to improve. I regained my confidence and got my independence back. My daughter and I moved into a home of our own, unfortunately I was not eligible for any assistance with getting the house, which I privately rented. We were truly blessed, which is a story for another time... I went on a hairdressing refresher course and my life got so much better.

Turning My Setbacks into My Biggest Comeback

My sister's business started to grow and get busy, she needed someone part-time to do some admin work for her. Meanwhile, the hours at the supermarket were just not working with my daughter, so I resigned and started working for my sister. We did not know how it was going to work out, two sisters working together! However, it was a real success! Unfortunately, six months later she was diagnosed with cancer and I had to step up and run her business. I did not do any of the life coaching, but I was having to deal with everything else and this was a time that really pushed me out of my comfort zone. It made me grow in so many ways and discover my passion and purpose in life.

Four years on, I am now the Business Operations Manager at my sister's coaching company. I oversee the whole business and support her and our clients. Our clients and the way we do business are extremely important to me personally and professionally. I have the freedom I want and I am able to work around my daughter meaning we can spend quality time together.

Alongside this, I have also rebuilt my hairdressing business and have some amazing clients. In November 2020, I launched a parenting and lifestyle blog, later this year I plan to publish my own book, as in my life I have faced many setbacks and, lastly, I will complete my grief coach qualification.

If I look back at my younger years, I cannot tell you how messy the journey has been, this is only a snippet. Sometimes it is hard not to feel like a failure, however, I am grateful for where I am today because it has helped me fulfil my purpose to help and inspire those who have also given up or had a setback in their life. I have learnt so many skills which I did not learn at college; it's all been self-taught, through perseverance and by declaring to myself that I wasn't going to feel like a failure anymore. Those challenging pages in my journal are now for me to look back at and reflect on how far I have come rather than ripping them out. The journey to get here has not been easy. But as I look back at everything I have achieved over the last 16 years of my career, it may be messy on paper but the positive impact and encouragement to others has been so worth it.

From Me to You

If we have not met before and you are reading this, wherever you are now, whether you are facing a redundancy, a career change, returning to work after being furloughed or no longer able to go back into your line of work due to the Covid pandemic. My own personal advice would be to allow yourself to GROW through this process and embrace it. You are designed with love and fearfully and wonderfully made. Please do not give up. Face those doubtful thoughts head on. Allow those setbacks to be your biggest comeback! You are never too old to start, to learn and to retrain! We get one chance at life and it is so full of opportunities. Make the most of it. I hope that this has been an encouragement to you. I am leaving you a few top tips I have learnt along this journey:

- Take time out and allow yourself to grieve.

- Accept what's happened, you can't change it.

- But forgive the situation and let it go.

- Focus on your attention on new beginnings.

- Learn from the lessons and allow them to help you grow.

- Always be grateful, no matter what and look for gratitude in those challenging times.

If you are struggling, or if you want to set up something for yourself, please reach out, we would love to help you.

I look forward to connecting with you.

"There's no shortage of remarkable ideas, what's missing is the will to execute them."

Seth Godin

ELIZABETH STANLEY

Earning a BSc Hons in Mathematics from Swansea University and graduating in 1999, Elizabeth started her career in hospitality. Everything started to change when she had her children in 2002 and 2005. Both times experiencing post-natal depression which led to her visiting a careers centre to get advice on her options. In 2008 she registered with USW Business School and started her studies to become a qualified Accountant.

Elizabeth qualified as an accountant in 2015, received her practice license in 2018 and started her own business, Stanley Finance, based in Newport the same year.

Connect with Elizabeth:

https://www.linkedin.com/in/elizabeth-stanley-20690b60/

https://www.twitter.com/FinanceStanley

https://www.facebook.com/StanleyFinanceAccountant

When Finance Calls

On such a warm sunny day, I have started to think back to where my career in accounts began—or rather nearly didn't.

From the beginning, I was always interested in accounts and finance. When in school I signed up for work experience in an accountancy practise and a presentation about accounting and IT.
The work experience office was rather dull and boring, filled with suits and separate offices with no chocolate in the fridge or milk for tea. I understood that this was just one company and put it aside, until I attended the presentation. Here I was faced with a very stiff-suited gentleman who spoke like a stereotypical accountant. He sounded so boring I combined this with the work experience and decided this was not the career for me. In fact, I actively fought against going into accountancy.

I carried on with my studies and went to university, graduating with a BSc Hons in Mathematics. It was here that I found my much-loved part-time job at a local hotel, which inspired my decision to pursue hospitality as a career. Over the next 14 years I had an exciting and varied career in hospitality. The roles I enjoyed most involved working with the public directly. I chose the roles that had a mix of front of house; for reservations, events and conferences, bar and restaurant; and the management side (which wasn't restricted to an office tucked away). For a long time no two days were the same. There was always a new contract to negotiate, new customers to look after and all manner of antics that the guests got up to (swimming pools in hotels and office parties are a drama magnet). The skills I took away with me included: not taking things personally, working with the public and realising that listening to what is being said is the key to being able to find out what the actual issue is.

Customer service is huge and there are so many areas embedded into that, being able to talk to and work with everyone is essential. As hospitality is a fast-moving and competitive industry, sticking to timescales and providing the information needed to make informed but fast decisions is essential. This is where my move into accounts began, I was always drawn to the numbers and 'what-ifs'. I loved budgets, the infamous accounts book was my favourite Sunday night task in one property. The numerous VAT rate changes meant I really had my work cut out for me, alongside my normal role, in another property. By this stage I realised I should revisit accountancy. I had become a mum of two amazing children and married a wonderful man. Both children were in school so we felt now was the time to look at what sort of career woman I wanted to be. As this was a huge change for us all, my first step was to visit a careers advisor to go through my options and see not only what was out there for me but also how much it cost. I was encouraged to attend an open day at USW Newport, which made my decision (local, reasonably priced per course and very supportive)—so began my studies at USW Newport Business School (one afternoon and evening a week) and a brand-new routine for the family.

During my studies I signed up with the careers team at USW knowing that gaining relevant experience was essential. In the third year of my studies, an amazing opportunity arose to work at the BBC in the finance team, based in Cardiff. I was successful with the application. During the interview they wanted lots of examples of varying situations. They knew that I came from a hospitality background but stressed that they wanted to see me tie those experiences to accounting.

During my period at the BBC I learned much more about accountancy as a career, I also completed my studies. Alongside my usual day-to-day role there were many additional opportunities to explore including earning a Blue Peter badge for hula hooping. Socialising via my new hobby opened up lots of other doors which were very unexpected. These included joining the staff choir as an accompanying musician playing the cornet. We performed in many locations including on the radio and at Llandaff cathedral—one of the many highlights was playing some sound effects for the autumn internationals one year.

To grow my career once qualified a promotion meant much travelling. So I made the difficult decision to look for a role closer to home.
I stayed in the industry, in that new role, for a few years after qualifying to increase my knowledge and experience. So that I could confidently run my own business and support others in running theirs.

In June 2018 I took the plunge and started my own accountancy practice. I collected the keys to office 13 on the 1st floor, above Newport Market and reality hit me hard. There was a lot of support from family and friends and potential clients had taken my business card and contact details. Other offices popped by to say hi and this is how I learned about #PortHour on a Monday night on Twitter (8pm every Monday). This is a simple way to network with other local businesses and develop some real relationships. This has had a really positive effect on the business increasing my professional local network, new customers, new suppliers and friends.

I spent the initial month making sure that all the start-up admin was up to date and networking events were booked. Good old-fashioned leg work helped me find my first client.

It is absolutely true what they say, once you have your first client, more follow. I believe this is due to your confidence growing. Personally, I have never looked back. I chose to be self-employed and I chose to concentrate on sole traders, partnerships and small businesses. I encourage everyone to have a free initial meeting with me (previously in the office, currently on video call) so that we can find out together what they really need and how we can make it work together.

Now I have been up and running for a few years, a few things I have learned are: be yourself—it is true that people buy from people and want to work with individuals. The more comfortable you are, the more confident you become and your ideal client becomes clearer (which is key).

Moving from employed to self-employed does generate a risk to your income BUT the real reason we take the step is to correct the work-life balance . Initially, to stabilise my income, I found a part-time temping job with a local company via a recruitment agency. This stability bought me some breathing space. The role finished around the same time that my business needed me full-time. Now I am at the stage where I will need another person with me if my business's growth continues as it has been—decisions need to be made as to what I really need next.

When we talk work-life balance no one really knows what this means. I found out in June 2019 when my husband had a stroke while we were in Exeter. Because I was self-employed I was able to arrange my diary around the needs of my family. My family and friends were amazing, my clients were amazing (and no deadlines were missed at all). The flexibility self-employment offered was amazing and meant I was where I needed to be, when I needed to be there. This has carried on since. A great friend advised me at the beginning to diary in family time and stick to it. It is so easy to get engrossed in your business because you believe that is what it is all about. Remember why you went self-employed.

A relaxed dress code isn't just welcomed, for me it is essential. I frequently get greeted with a relieved nervous smile and the comment, "phew, you look human".
Whilst 9am-5pm might sound lovely, however, when everyone works the same hours, this can hamper the support offered. I happily arrange calls and meetings after regular office hours (at a reasonable time of course), after all, I control my own diary.

I have an IT professional (my husband) in the family, who has made sure I am securely connected to what I need, where I need it. My eldest has recently started her university journey. She is brilliant with design, so I have brought her on board with me to help with this side of the business.

March 2020 changed many things for all of us. My office was closed, so I uprooted, brought home everything I needed and started working from my dressing table. During the summer a major development was confirmed and

I had to find a new office altogether. Thanks to the amazing network I had built up, I am now based in a manor house at the top of a Victorian park, 10 minutes' walk away from home. A great upgrade.

During this period, business has grown. The demand on accountants has been huge due to the many changes that affect all businesses and individuals. Staying on top of everything has been challenging, but what I have found works best is to focus on what my clients need to be aware of and to know who the best contacts are to signpost where more specialised support is needed (funding as an example is shared between HMRC, Business Wales and local councils).

Starting Stanley Finance, supporting the businesses I have and watching the growth and development of many has been the best and most exciting journey to date. For my family and I, it has been the best decision with lots more to come.

"I don't know the word 'quit.' Either I
never did, or I have abolished it."

Susan Butcher

HELEN FARMER

Helen is an Inclusion and Impact Consultant/Coach and social mobility expert, specialising in the research, design, strategy and set up of multi-partner projects and programmes, both in the UK and overseas. She supports and creates programmes and spaces for frank conversations from school to boardroom, helping people transform their individual agency and influence for helping more underrepresented people feel like they belong.

Helen also works as a speaker, activist and writer for inclusion and impact, especially for women in business and mental health and wellbeing. Helen has plans to write children's books and create and curate art to help disrupt the status quo for exploring and listening to lived experience.

Contact and connect with Helen:

Email: Helen@voicebyvolume.com

https://www.LinkedIn.com/in/Helenfarmer

https://www.twitter.com/helen_farmer

https://www.instagram.com/helen_farmer

From Rock Bottom to Bouncing Back – Belonging in My Work for Inclusion

Warning: this story describes an attack

I want you to know it's going to be ok. I want you to know it's ok to feel what you feel in any moment. I want you to know that you're enough already, and that you belong in yourself.

You have power and you control how you react, even though you can't control other people or events, their actions and reactions.

Life can be lonely, hard, difficult and overwhelming and you may feel like you can't cope with even one more tiny little thing.

It's ok. It's normal to feel like that or whatever else you're feeling.

Unfortunately, it isn't unique. But there are people, places, communities and books, where you can find like-minded people with similar lived experience, to help you work through your stuff, especially the hard stuff.

This is my story about what helped me, what didn't, what I wish I'd known and what I would say to myself back then. I'm going to share a bit of me, my story, and how that's driven me and drives me to make work and workplaces better for everyone.

Ultimately, I want to help more people belong in themselves.

Baby Number One and Returning to Work

Everything changed for me when I went back to work after my first maternity leave in October 2010, to a struggle that lasted two years.

I went back to a job that hadn't been covered, a manager who was retiring and a colleague who was leaving to work somewhere else. Back to a bit of a vacuum where my job and my identity had been. I remember a colleague saying you lose yourself a bit when you have a baby. That identity change from being an individual to being a mother and carer.

The whole organisation was restructuring. There was a lot of change and a lot of challenge.

And I felt lost.

Don't get me wrong, the first few days when I got back were fine, nice even. I went to an event, saw people I'd not seen for a while, was told to take my time.

But it wasn't long before I settled into some kind of nothing. Wondering what to do and where did I belong?

PTSD

After a couple of months, on the eve of my husband's 40th birthday, we heard a really strange noise outside our house in the middle of the night. We looked out of the window. Someone was being attacked. We called the police. A man in the dark holding a woman in a headlock walking along the street. Shouting. Holding her against a car. Hands round her neck. All the while we were talking to the police as our baby slept in the other room.

It was scary.

Five police cars and an ambulance appeared. By this time the man was sat on top of the woman after having throttled her. It was around the time Jo Yates was murdered and they hadn't found anyone yet, maybe that made the police come quicker. I don't know. But it was horrible.

The good news is the woman was all right.

Apparently, he was her husband and he hadn't had his medicine which helped him with his mental health. She wanted to thank us but I didn't really want to be known to them. I wanted to be anonymous, with my family and a small baby. I had to walk in the same streets where these people lived.

Around that time, I just felt this heavy, thick, black fog come over me. And a big, black hole of fear near me, surrounding me. I later found the label, PTSD (Post-Traumatic Stress Disorder). For me it was a feeling of this fog and fear. I went into work with that feeling, alongside not being sure what my identity was anymore.

Getting Signed Off With Stress

At work I moved around departments but felt really stressed. I thought the problem was with my manager, with someone else. But then an HR person told me I should go and see the doctor so I did. I got signed off work.

I wondered if I wasn't working, then what was I going to do?

I still had the baby at home most of the time but they did go into nursery as well.

So I followed the course of support, the options available to me through the general practitioner, with my 'stress and anxiety' label.

CBT - Cognitive Behaviour Therapy/ Mindfulness/ Stress Workshops

I told the counsellors and psychotherapists what they, and I, wanted to hear. I did stress workshops. I got stressed about going to the stress workshops and stressed that I was getting stressed about the stress workshops! But looking back, I feel like I got a 30-year head start on the other people in the stress workshops, they seemed to be in their 60s and 70s.

The CBT was a series of 1:1 support, a combination of the expert listening to me, offering tools I could use to help me be more aware of myself and my thoughts, and how to manage them.

Mindfulness was, and continues to be, one of the most helpful tools and practices I learned. I gave in to the discomfort of lying or sitting in a community hall with other (stressed) people, and listened to the calm voice and sounds the leader led us through. Perhaps the biggest breakthrough was starting to listen to my body and breathing, even simply adjusting my shoulders down when tense or noticing the tension in my stomach helped. The focus on the absolute simplicity and necessity of breath continues to help me too. And even a few minutes of noticing your breath can help, when you remember.

The stress workshops weren't a therapy session sharing the pain, but sessions to help explore the different facets of our lives through tools that could help us to manage what we could physically and mentally do, to help ourselves and to change things up a bit. To explore and change thought patterns and behaviours that didn't help us, and treat ourselves more kindly along the way.

Redundancy

Then what? After two years in this no man's (or woman's) land of restructuring I moved departments, fought for my job, to keep my place in the hierarchy, in the system. I did my best. But I got undermined and my self-esteem was on the floor, rock bottom.

There were a few friendly faces around but to be honest, I'd resisted the social side of things. As quite a private, introverted person, I put up walls. And I wasn't ready to let them down.

Someone on my team started undermining me, telling others not to do what I'd asked them to do. I tried to talk to them about dignity at work. They said, "There is no dignity at work". We had mediators to try and help us. Whilst I wasn't the most straightforward person to deal with then, they didn't help me the best either. Eventually one morning I got shown a PowerPoint presentation. This is the structure of the team. Your job is not in it. They didn't use these words but it felt like they were saying you don't exist anymore, you're not needed.

I cried.

I really cried.

My manager offered to get my bag but I said no. I wasn't afraid to cry by this point, my mindfulness teacher told me it is ok to cry, anywhere, even at work. She helped me give myself permission to feel, so I cried my way back to my desk, picked my bag up and left. They had a meeting that afternoon that I didn't have to go to, but I did. Now everyone else, perhaps 40 people, got to see the diagram without my job, without me in it.

They asked if anyone had any questions or comments. Talk about tumbleweed and awkward! I put my hand up and spoke up. I said, "I hope no one else has to go through what I've been through or feel what I've felt, it's been the hardest time of my life."

And that was it.

A looooong two years. Done.

So What Happened Next?

In 2013 I went on garden leave and signed on. Off I went to the Jobcentre. My three-year-old asked if it was my new office. I just said yes.

I remember the job advisor counting up the actions I had to do one week— 1, 2…38 things by this time next week. I didn't do them. Getting to the Jobcentre once a week was a lot.

I needed a new approach so I switched to the 'New Enterprise Scheme', got a coach/advisor to help me explore my vision. I shared some of the stuff I'd done online with this amazing Aspire community, about what I wanted to do, who I was and what I was excited about. I started to create a business as a Catalyst and Connector, heading into the Brave Office in St. Paul's (Bristol) with my daughter in the buggy and, by that stage, pregnant with my next child.

At the same time, I started to panic about needing work. Should I work in a pub and get a bit tired? I'm pregnant. It's not good for the baby. Should I be a cleaner? But will the chemicals harm the baby?

Luckily, I started to find some work, at first in the Schumacher Institute facilitating workshops (thanks Ian Roderick, you're an amazing, kind and clever person).

And then I got not one but two jobs. One of them with a technology company in the Bristol and Bath Science Park and another one at Gateway to Research (https://gtr.ukri.org/). This was my first experience as a contractor and what it was like to be different (perhaps treated as less than an employee by the system), as well as being treated really well by the people I worked with directly.

Baby Number Two

Next up? Baby number two arrives! Statutory Maternity Pay (self-employed) runs out fast. Thankfully I was introduced to the amazing Faye Dicker, her bump a month ahead of mine, and the Freelance Mum community she was about to give birth to. I made it to the first Freelance Mum networking event, late. At Bristol Harbour I could see a small army of mums walking back to the SS Great Britain. I gatecrashed a photo for the papers. I had found a tribe where I belonged.

New Business, New Skills, New Baby and New Me

I found the strength to learn new skills and try some new things. I got to grips with (new-fangled) things like Mail Chimp and Eventbrite. Work arrived too:

- An event project with Paola, of Paola Davis Events, and Mel Bound, now of This Mum Runs.
- A stint as newsletter writer for Freelance Mum.

Other exciting events and things followed, often taking baby with me, sometimes I asked, sometimes I didn't. Most people didn't mind (some people were horrified) at a bit of breastfeeding in the John Lewis café.

I got to see different parts of Bristol:

- Working with David Pick and young people age 16 to 25 in a business in Lawrence Weston. I watched their confidence rise throughout the course. Despite the bravado, they were simply doing their best.

- Helping set up the community and supporting partners for the entrepreneurs' programme with social or environmental goals as part of Ecopreneurs with Steve Clark.
- Working with Noha Nasser, and people from all across the public, private and third sector of our city as part of Bridging Cultures. We even had Marvin Rees, Mayor, and Kalpna Woolf, with their respective One City and 91 Ways approaches.

I tried to get into places I thought I wanted to be, in the technology and corporate business world, pitching and interviewing, but it didn't work. Set Squared? Nope. NatWest incubator? Nope. (That one was like my X Factor—I tried that three times, I think.)

So where did I feel welcome? Desklodge and Thanh Quan-Nichols welcomed me with open arms. Also, Women's Tech Hub, Serrie Chapman and Susie King.

I got to do an unconscious bias talk on 'Why women are underrepresented in engineering.' at University of Bristol, and later went on to work with them on a School to Boardroom event at Bristol Tech Fair with WISE - Women in Science and Engineering.

For nearly three years I've been working at Ablaze Bristol, a charity to help level the playing field for children and teenagers who don't get the same opportunities just because of where they live and their backgrounds.

Last year, with Legacy Strategies Ltd, I got to work with a construction company in London on the Parliament estate, helping with their leadership and strategy for inclusion.

What Helped?

In understanding my values, I found my purpose. In finding my purpose, I found places and roles where I thrive. I wanted my experience to become a catalyst for change. In finding my tribes, I found my strength to speak up.

Communities

I explored and started up communities in Bristol. Bristol chapters of these amazing organisations supporting people with purpose:

- Escape the City, helping people find or create work they love, with purpose
- Urbanistas, UK, a women-led leadership group making cities better for everyone
- Prowess Connect, InvestinWomen, 2015.

Exploring and supporting online communities massively helped me find a sense of self and possibility. I encourage you to do the same, to both challenge and support yourself.

The Inside Work

As an imperfect, white privileged human, I continue to do the inner work. I've been on more courses than you can shake a stick at, some of them I even completed. Having experienced my own feelings of exclusion in the workplace, here I am in 2021, having helped to design and deliver an inclusion programme for over 50 creative businesses. It was my ideal job when I started in February 2020, and a couple of weeks later we locked down for the pandemic. Despite a shaky start, wondering what the hell to do and how to do it, with the support and expertise of the partners in the Watershed and University of the West of England, and a creative technologist (Abbie Freeman) joining our team, we went online. Helping lots of people on their personal and organisational leadership journey.

And I'm about to tackle the Digital Engineering and Technology sector, big areas of need and possibility for better inclusion and workplaces for everyone.

What I Learned About Me and Our Society

Your experience is valid. Sometimes you have to 'be your own golden nugget' (Change Catalyst Conference 2018). I have used my experience to campaign for better work and workplaces for women, and my consultancy focusses on better workplaces for everyone.

We need to take the brakes off (skills) with tailored training and support for women's enterprise. We keep being told to celebrate another business, incubator or scheme specially for women or specially for people of colour, or join in with the latest female 'role model' search. But imagine if overrepresented people simply included them in the first place?

Childcare remains an issue, especially for single parents, as noted by Joeli Brierly in her new book 'Pregnant Then Screwed', and Joeli continues lobbying for better support for parents.

So My Latest Career Change? Where Am I Bouncing Off to Next?

Number five on the 2015 Manifesto for Women in Business—investment in funding—women need a fair share of government support. With 21 percent of women having faced redundancy or having to leave work due to caring responsibilities in 2020-2021, during the COVID-19 pandemic, the gaps are more like chasms now. I'm off to explore frank conversations asking for data about where the time, money and resources are going and not going, especially in the name of 'growth' and 'jobs' and 'productivity'.

I still get my highs and my lows and my nos. And I am addicted to stories and learning, often within the safety and support of a book or community. Even if sometimes I'm a little bit scared, almost feeling a little guilty or embarrassed about my latest learning crush, it has all been worth it, and leads me on to the next thing.

"Far and away the best prize that life offers is the chance to work hard at work worth doing."

Theodore Roosevelt

JASON CONWAY

Jason Conway is a Stroud-based, award-winning creative professional; Designer, Artist, Photographer, Poet, Writer and Creative Mentor. He uses his love of nature and passion for creative expression, to educate and inspire others to make a positive difference in the world. Jason is a published author and poet, he is one of two directors of The Gloucestershire Poetry Society and part of arts collective, Studi3stroud. Jason launched his new arts magazine, Steel Jackdaw, in January 2021.

He loves natural, home cooked food, escaping into nature, for natural mindfulness and inspiration, and adventures with his partner Michelle and rescue dog Foxy.

Find and connect with Jason:

https://www.thedaydreamacademy.com

https://www.facebook.com/TheDaydreamAcademy

https://www.twitter.com/Daydreamacademy

https://www.instagram.com/jasonleeconway

https://www.linkedin.com/in/jasonleeconway

Permission to Dream

You could say that I'm the eternal daydreamer and you'd be right! I've spent a great deal of my life daydreaming and I make no apologies for that. Why? Well, as it happens it's turned out to be the route of my success.

Back in my wide-eyed and impressionable school days, I was often blissfully lost in my own world; chasing dragons, being a superhero, a wizard or pirate or exploring space. Needless to say, my early school reports were frequented with comments of 'having his head in the clouds', 'needing to pay more attention' and 'being too easily distracted'. The education system didn't cater for daydreamers. I wanted to draw, dream stories, paint, think, question, make and play.

My spare time was spent mostly outside, in all weathers, exploring my local town and its green and wild spaces. I'd walk or cycle around looking to see what was around the next corner, down alleyways, behind hedges, across playing fields, through tunnels and wooded areas, on roofs. Places that most people didn't look. I'd watch the clouds go by, crawl on my hands and knees in search of tiny worlds, hide in bushes and watch through leaves. I'd explore building sites and derelict warehouses, look under rocks and fallen branches, or dig for treasure! Sometimes as the narrator but mostly happily chatting with imaginary characters; conversing with flowers, bugs, trees and the occasional stone too. I look back now and feel sorry for my mother, who'd often tell me off for disappearing for the whole day and coming back filthy. Who could blame her? I have a very fond memory of lying in a huge puddle on an empty side street. It was cold but I loved the feeling, free to float and gaze at the sky. My father loved to fix things and that gave me permission to disassemble objects and figure out how they'd go back together. They sometimes didn't. I'd imagine myself being tiny, walking over circuit boards, through glowing glass bulbs (when TVs had them inside), being part of miniature plastic and metal worlds.

Art college was a wonderland for me, filled with experimentation and creative play but I had a pre-career bounce-back to get there. During the last few years at school, I didn't have an idea of what I wanted to do for a career (I'd be very surprised if anyone really does). I did poorly in my exams, having mental blocks and I can remember feeling lost when I saw my grades and clueless of what job I'd like to do. Thankfully, my father dug out a folder of my sketches (I drew incessantly) and took them to the art teacher who was baffled that I hadn't taken art as an option. She recommended that I go to art college. Thanks to the initiative of my father, I realised I should be doing something creative in my life. As it turned out, I excelled at college and vowed to myself that I would find a creative job.

Fast-forward to my university years. Whilst wonderful, they ended with a similar feeling of loss and another bounce-back. The coursework became far too limited in scope and my creative expression was stifled. I felt I was battling the system. The saving grace came from my Apple Mac lecturer, who had become a friend. I remember chatting with him about the situation and he said that I should pursue a career in graphic design. He'd taken the time to get to know his students and spotted something in my work. For a second time, I took a pit stop and accepted the guidance of a 'gatekeeper' to show me a path.

After graduating, the first three years were spent working in a warehouse, picking orders and stocktaking. I filled the boredom of repetitive work by making extra money as an artist, drawing portraits, painting T-Shirts, illustrating and designing a few tattoos. I can remember telling my boss that I'd make a career for myself as an artist or designer and seeing his less than supportive reaction. I loved the day when I told my boss that I'd got a job as an artist. The new job involved painting resin figurines but it turned out to be yet more repetitive work.

I searched for art and design jobs in the local newspaper and spotted a tiny advert for a graphic designer. The job turned out to be technical drawing for a leading kiln manufacturer. Thankfully, I'd done lots of that at uni and I got the job. It was interesting work with job satisfaction and a great atmosphere. During my time there, I overheard that the department used to have an Apple Mac that had stopped working and was left in the warehouse. I found it and brought it back into the office, took it apart, gave it a clean and it worked just fine. That was the day I officially became a graphic designer. I was put in charge of designing the company's internal documents and trade magazine adverts. Four months later, a marketing director joined the firm and gave me an assistant marketing role. I became the company photographer too, and just before I left that job I designed and project managed a new reception area. This job had given me the freedom and autonomy to be self-directed.

Great things don't always last and after hearing a rumour that the company was going into liquidation, I returned to the newspapers and saw a graphic design job being advertised. I joined the marketing team at the UK's biggest independent distributor of photography products and was immersed in graphic projects and marketing duties. I had a lot of freedom to manage my days. I demonstrated early digital cameras and scanners at trade and public exhibitions, designed internal and external marketing, show stands and learned about professional cameras from one of the staff there. About a year into this 'dream job', I was asked if I'd be interested in joining their technical team to provide Apple support to retail customers. While I loved the current role, I said yes to embrace the change of direction. They knew that I knew an Apple Mac inside and out but it wasn't a good move. I spent my days on the phone helping people to fix their software issues and explaining how to use digital cameras and scanners. I missed the design work and it hit home that I'd made a mistake that was draining me. So, I handed in my notice and said goodbye to a wonderful company with a great reputation and team. Time for yet another bounce-back.

This time, I focussed on finding freelance work and a school friend let me share a small office, in his rug shop, to work from. It turned out that I was a pretty good rug seller. I soon landed a regular client, a local rug distributor, photographing their rugs, designing their new logo and advertising. I also freelanced with a local print company to help with design tasks and ended up being trusted to manage the design office and even the company on one occasion, when the MD was on holiday. I got to know the print industry inside out, everything I would need to succeed as a designer.

I thrived freelancing. I learned how to code and design websites, write copy and many more creative skills over the years, all self-directed and I drifted along blissfully.

In 2008, I moved from Staffordshire to Gloucester for love, excited but a little scared at having to restart my business again. I was part of a loving family unit (myself, my partner, daughter and stepdaughter) and the work rolled in. Fast-forward to 2016 and the relationship ended. We moved to Spain, to see if we could make a new start in a new country but I struggled to cope with the split and moved back to the UK on my own. My world crumbled with my daughter and stepdaughter in Spain and I struggled from day to day with the grief of separation and the added pressure of having to make a new start back in Gloucester. I'd let go of most of my clients whilst in Spain, as I'd hoped to start a career as an artist over there and had very few possessions to my name (we'd decluttered and sold everything ready for the Spanish move).

This period turned out to be the most difficult bounce-back and the most challenging of my life. I started losing weight, neglected myself, had low self-esteem and felt lost and empty. Thankfully, I'd been filled with some inspirational books over the previous few years. From professional and personal development to job and lifestyle hacking, and whilst I endured the suffering of loss, I knew I had to get out and make things happen and I did just that. I joined walking groups for fitness, networking groups for business and regular nature escapes that fuelled my inspiration and boosted my well-being and mental health.

One month after moving back, a friend ask if I'd like to join his new poetry group on Facebook. I said yes immediately, to enjoy the new challenge. Those books had taught me to say yes to new opportunities and face my fears. I'd little experience of poetry. The only serious poem I'd ever written was in July, earlier that year. On a family holiday in Woolacombe, Devon, I had an epiphany whilst swimming in the sea and rushed back to the accommodation we stayed in and was compelled to write. That poem would become a hidden premonition of separation and drifting apart. I dived head first into writing poems and quickly fell in love with writing. It brought me solace, an escape, allowing me to regain the creative spark that had been suppressed by grief. It felt like I'd found a new purpose in life and the creativity bloomed. I faced my fear of public speaking by going to open mic events, taking the stage to read and I quickly caught the 'stage bug'. I also gained a new family, a family of poets.

Race forward to today, and I'm a co-director of The Gloucestershire Poetry Society, a published poet who performs at festivals, for businesses and online poetry events. I judge competitions, run workshops and mentor other poets. I have a new passion and path to follow and I love it!

Poetry is the spark that's renewed my love of creative expression and gifted me a new life, filled with wonderful opportunities. It's revived my love of design and boosted my business with a new way of thinking to create ideas. I'm also a book cover designer, through my links with poets and writers. The strength that poetry performance has given me has enabled me to have the confidence to become a website trainer. It's given me permission to explore writing as a career with a globe of possibilities.

I've bounced back quite a few times in my life, each navigating me back to a career as a creative. Through self-learning, luck, stubbornness, 'gatekeepers' and being fearless, I can smile when I say to people that I'm a professional daydreamer! In fact, I changed my business name to The Daydream Academy in October 2020. In January this year, I started my own arts magazine called Steel Jackdaw to celebrate the power of creative expression, champion the arts and give back to charity. Not bad work for a 'head in the clouds' type of guy!

Daydreaming has been invaluable to my development. It's the very essence of creativity. I hope, with a passion, that the arts will be given equal importance to academic subjects, as they gift people so much pleasure, reflection, inspiration, curiosity and the time to dream. Not to mention their huge boost to the UK economy.

I wish you all the time to daydream, once in a while, but be careful, it may just change your life!

"If you really look closely, most overnight successes took a long time."

Steve Jobs

KERRY BELLAMY

Kerry is a certified Coach and Trainer with a passion for helping her clients create balance and achieve their potential and is known for her friendly and holistic approach. With a wide range of practical experience in business, leadership, service management and personal/professional development, she holds her clients to account, tackles their overwhelm and helps them to create more resourceful patterns, all with a smile. She is a mother, wife, proud self-employed business owner and insatiable learner. Kerry walks alongside her clients to support them in becoming the successful, balanced and amazing individuals they truly are.

Find and connect with Kerry:

https://www.kerrybellamy.com

https://www.instagram.com/kbbalancecoach

https://www.facebook.com/KerryBCoaching

https://www.linkedin.com/in/kerrybellamy/

A Self-Employed Self-Growth Adventure

I first started working at the age of 15, as a Saturday girl at a local barber shop. I would take phone bookings, sweep floors and occasionally wash clients' hair. It wasn't much, but it was mine and I felt so proud of myself for having a job and being able to save my own money. From there on I always had a job. I've been a waitress, a bartender, an events organiser, theatre front-of-house, telesales, receptionist and ice cream seller; all before I finished university.

After I got married, at the ripe old age of 23, both hubby and I worked full-time in the day and switched between two evening jobs at the same time. I never really thought much of it, other than we were able to pay the bills and treat ourselves every now and then.

I have always been employed, whether it was temporary agency contracts that started off as, "Go here for a week" and quickly extended into 6–12-month roles as Admin Assistant, Receptionist and Sales Support. I even tried banking for a short time. Or later into long-term employment for two to five years at a time in roles like Team Leader, Client Consultant, Head of Department and Service Manager. I had an overriding belief that, if I wanted work, I could get it. Being employed is, or was, a huge part of who I was.

Fast-forward to my late 30s, and the company I was working for announced that they were heading into merger talks. As the plans progressed, it emerged that many existing roles would likely be duplicated. No one really knew what to expect, the dreaded R-words started to surface; redeployment and redundancy. And, as we were the smaller of the two organisations, everything seemed stacked in the other guy's favour. I decided to sit tight, watch and wait for more information before making any decisions; but I had a quiet plan.

You see, I had always secretly dreamed of being my own boss, running my own company. It was just that my financial resources and practical know-how were somewhat limited. And by now we had two young children to provide for, so it didn't seem right to throw caution to the wind. However, I did have irons in the fire and worked hard on creating connections and building my network.

A couple of years earlier I had started working as the Mentor Manager at the local university. When I took over the role there was half a dozen students involved. By the time we got to the merger talks, there were over 70 students working for me. Out of all the roles I'd ever had, this one hit all my happy buttons. I believed in the service and what we were contributing to the student experience. I loved the people I was working with (many of them are still close friends) and I had a clear vision of how we could continue to scale up at speed; to support even more students after the merger. This, however, was not to be the case.

I remember the email landing in my inbox. Would I like to apply for voluntary severance? My stomach dropped, what did this mean? They were looking to reduce staff numbers by offering a severance package to those who 'jumped ship early' (as one colleague put it). I realised I needed to shift my attention from drawing up lofty plans for service growth and start to really listen to the business conversations that were happening around me. I needed to get a sense of what the appetite really was for this kind of service, a service I had poured my heart and soul into for five years. I realised that, even with all the creative ideas and best intentions, any service still surviving in the new era would be vastly different to what we had worked so hard to build. Staying in this role would mean taking a five-year backwards step and there was no guarantee that I would ever be able to create the same offering again in the future. I had a choice to make and I needed to know *all* my options.

A few short months later I was sat in a hotel restaurant eating a lovely meal and discussing the possibility of me leaving employment and becoming a freelance trainer and business partner in a training company. It felt somewhat surreal, seriously scary but also hugely exciting. Not long after that dinner, I heard more about the intended plans for my employed role and, as a result, my severance package was agreed. But by this point I already knew what I wanted, and I delivered my first freelance training workshop six weeks later. It was a beautifully sunny day and as I drove home after the session, I had the windows down and the radio up, feeling like I could take on the world.

I had so much to learn about running a business and being a trainer, the months whipped by as I launched myself into my new career wholeheartedly. I gathered new skills, knowledge and experiences. I was lucky enough to travel and work in Paris, Munich, Switzerland and Amsterdam as well as all over the UK. I took on solo delivery projects and had the wonderful experience of co-facilitating and being able to witness someone else's talent and skill. And, whilst doing all of this I was also learning how to run a business, make sales and tackle company finances. Friends would tell me how envious they were of my new 'high-flying' life. How they wished they could stay in hotels and have someone else cook for them and make their bed. How we must be financially stable now because of the day rate I was able to charge. It was exhilarating, and it was exhausting.

Don't misunderstand me, I absolutely loved my new career, and I was experiencing so much that I knew would keep me interested and excited for years to come. What's more, I was now the master of my own destiny; I could choose when and where I worked, what projects to get involved with and who I worked with. Coffee shops became my office space, and I didn't have to ask anyone for time off to go to a school play or sports day. The ability to be completely in control of my time was so freeing. I even became an avid audiobook listener, ticking off trilogies, multiple series and even the odd autobiography, as I clocked up hundreds of miles each month travelling to and from delivery sessions.

However, although I was theoretically master of my own time, my husband and I had to quickly learn how to juggle two new careers (he had also recently retrained), two children, a house and a crazy diary that saw me staying away from home, sometimes for a few nights at a time, for the first time since we'd been married. My friends had been right, it was lovely to be able to stay in hotels and having someone else do all the cooking. However, it comes nowhere close to the joy of sliding into your own bed and snuggling up with the love of your life.

What I also hadn't fully anticipated was the strange niggling sensation of being somehow adrift. After all, in so many ways I was thriving; my cup was filled up every time I saw a participant achieve their elusive 'a-ha' moment, my income was good, and I had a solid pipeline of work for the months ahead. Yet something deep inside me still felt ever so slightly off kilter. It only seemed to bubble to the surface in the quiet reflective moments, but I couldn't quite put my finger on what it was.

I finally realised that what was off was my sense of identity, who I saw myself as, now that I was no longer employed. 'Freelancer' felt too frivolous, 'business partner' felt too grandiose, 'trainer' felt like a toy without a home. I needed to claim myself in some way.

It wasn't until the subject of me becoming employed by the training business came up some years later that I had my first 'a-ha' moment. In that moment, when I was directly asked to consider employment again, every fibre in my being screamed, "No". It was such an immediate gut reaction, it shocked me. When asked to explain, I couldn't give a clear answer, I just knew I didn't want it. Now please understand, I believe wholeheartedly in this business and I truly value and respect the work and the people in it. So why didn't I want to be employed?

Over the years that have followed I am proud to say that I continued to work in the same business, we went through our own merger and now have offices in three countries. This has in fact been one of the longest careers I have ever had in my life and I see no signs of wanting to have it come to an end any time soon. I have grown so much, and I am still learning, even now some nine years later. I've trained and coached thousands of people, travelled all over the UK and Europe and overcome many of my limiting beliefs along the way. I am not the same person I was when I started the wild ride of freelancing. I have learnt to find balance, to say yes when it suits my life goals and no when it drains me. I no longer feel the need to be guilty when putting boundaries in place and protecting what is important to me and my family. Without those boundaries I know I can become overwhelmed and emotionally drained; I know that my relationships will suffer and the undermining voice in my head gets to play on its soapbox. In that state I'm no fun to be around and I'm certainly not able to bring out the best in myself or my participants. I have learned to work hard when I want to and to chill hard when I need to.

If you are someone who has either found yourself in a world turned upside down through job loss or you have a sneaking suspicion you have a business inside of you waiting to be created, then consider stepping out on your own and going on a crazy, wild adventure. It's a rollercoaster of awesomely amazing and super scary moments and there is nothing quite like it. You will learn more about yourself in six months of working for yourself than you will ever learn working for someone else. A word or two of advice as you take those first steps; pause for a moment to consider your whole life, ask yourself what fills you up and what zaps your energy and agree with yourself that finding your version of balance is key to your success.

As for me, I'm pleased to say that I have finally claimed myself; I am self-employed. It's the best job in the world.

"Almost everything worthwhile carries with it some sort of risk, whether it's starting a new business, whether it's leaving home, whether it's getting married, or whether it's flying into space."

Chris Hadfield

MARIA NEWMAN

Known as Mummy on a Break and the founder of The Busy Working Mums club, helping mums is what Maria does.

She loves working with mums who feel like they are watching their life from the sidelines, Maria provides the tools and techniques, together with tough love, to get them moving in the right direction.

Maria lives in Bristol with her husband and two energetic children. In her spare time, she likes to run whilst listening to Audible books, is a blue belt in kick boxing martial arts, loves cooking/eating/talking about food and dances and sings like nobody's watching!

Learn more about and connect with Maria:

Email: Mummyonabreak@outlook.com

https://www.facebook.com/MummyOnABreak

https://www.instagram.com/mummyonabreak

https://www.pinterest.co.uk/mummyonabreakMaria/

https://www.anchor.fm/mummyonabreak

https://www.youtube.com/channel/UClEhv_9PngF-jQHiuBI1pkg

https://www.linkedin.com/in/maria-newman/

https://www.twitter.com/MariaAndreasNe1

https://www.mummyonabreak.co.uk

There's No Such Thing as the Right Time

Would you leave a successful career, working for a well-respected company, whilst on maternity leave with baby number two and without a plan?

One of my earliest memories in my career is driving up to Uxbridge University to recruit some university students for internships at Rolls-Royce. I was accompanying a senior manager and, like most people, I wanted to know his story. It wasn't unusual. He'd started as an apprentice and gradually worked his way up through the ranks. Before he knew it, he'd got married, had children and was now at the age where the pension was too good for him to leave the company.

Oh my goodness. That's when it hit me. My immediate response was I am never going to be in a position like that. I decided there and then that I was not going to work for anyone for longer than five years. There was no way I was going to put myself in a position where I felt locked in.

Well, fast-forward 17 years and I was in danger of turning into that person. Five years turned to 10 years, 10 years turned to 15 years and so on. I was married, I had a beautiful daughter and I was heavily pregnant with baby number two.

Don't get me wrong, I had a great career at Rolls-Royce. I worked on some really interesting projects.

Like being part of the team that managed the build of the new production factory at Filton, whilst simultaneously transferring the production team and equipment from the old site to the new site. I have such fond memories of this project. The team was great and what we achieved was amazing.

The most challenging point in my career was when I project managed an engineering development programme. This really tested me. I had many sleepless nights. I mean there was me, a non-engineer, leading a team of highly qualified engineering professionals. I definitely remember feeling out of my comfort zone. But at the end of the day, we delivered what was necessary to the customer and it felt amazing!

And then finally, the last project that I worked on was probably one of my greatest achievements. I took this plain, uninspiring and massive office space that was occupied by 200 individuals and I led the team who turned it into a modern, versatile workspace that our colleagues would enjoy working in. It had splashes of colour and encouraged different types of working styles. It made working feel more sociable and comfortable. It was just different from the other workspaces on site and I felt really proud of what we had achieved.

But… The fact was, I still kept thinking about that moment in the car when I first started at Rolls-Royce. Now, more than ever, I thought I was in danger of being stuck in this company until retirement. And like the thousands of other times I'd remembered that initial conversation, I was questioning what I was doing. This wasn't the first time I had felt like I was in the wrong career. This wasn't the first time I had realised I wasn't supposed to be doing this. I knew something needed to change. But, unlike the other times I was beginning to think the time *was* right. And, unlike other times I *did* feel brave enough to make that change.

However, it wasn't until I was about to go on maternity leave to have my baby boy, baby number two, that I really started thinking about where I was and where I wanted to go. Although maternity leave was imminent, I kept on thinking about what I was going to come back to afterwards. And I just couldn't face the thought of coming back. Coming back to this career.

You see, I sort of fell into working for Rolls-Royce. It wouldn't have necessarily been my first choice. But it was a good company. Great benefits. I'd have job security. And it was just up the road from my family home. My parents were delighted. So, it seemed like the obvious choice.

To be honest, I actually dreamed of working for a more forward-thinking company. One that provided a service or made a product that I knew more about and one that I was passionate about. Aeroplane engines are impressive but they're not really my thing.

The more I thought about what I was coming back to after maternity leave, the more I thought I didn't want to come back. But what *would* I do if I didn't come back? Rolls-Royce was all I'd ever known. Well, other than working for my dad in our seaside restaurant.

It was too late; the seed was planted. Over the following months, all I could think about was what would be next?

Fortunately, whilst I was on maternity leave, the company was going through a redundancy programme. I saw this as the perfect opportunity to break free and to really go for what I wanted. Sort of.

What made this decision even more important was that although my children at that point were very little, I wanted to be a good role model for them. I wanted them to go after their dreams. I wanted to encourage them to go after what they wanted. But how could I do that for them if I wasn't willing to do it for myself? So, the decision was made and with the support of my husband, I decided to take voluntary redundancy.

But I didn't really have a plan on what I was going to do next!

All I knew was I was going to take 2017 as a year to consciously decide what I wanted to do next. That was the only thing that I had planned. Crazy? Brave? At that point all I knew was it felt right.

So, 2017 was set to be my big adventure and to help me record my highs and lows I decided to set up my 'Mummy on a Break' Facebook page. I wanted to use the opportunity to maybe inspire other mums to also be brave. Not necessarily leave their jobs but be more aware as to what their wants and needs were, other than being an amazing mum.

It was so liberating having a year off. A year to try different things out. See what direction I wanted to go in.

I started volunteering for the Children's Hospital once a week for a couple of hours. I set up the Little Elves Festive Fair in support of CLIC Sargent.

One of the most important things I did was to work with a life coach, Anna.

Until I started working with Anna, I didn't realise that I was wearing blinkers. I was not seeing all the opportunities that were available to me.

Anna questioned nearly all the assumptions that I'd been making about what I could and should do. She got me thinking about what was possible. And it's thanks to her that I even considered starting my journey as a business owner.

One of the first things she asked me was, "What do you really want to do?" My answer; I wanted to start my own business. But I didn't have an idea. Wow. I didn't see that one coming. Over the next few months, it became clear that I definitely wanted to start my own business. Why? I found myself looking at job ads and not feeling inspired whatsoever. Besides, retirement was still 25 years away. That's a long time, and there was no way I was going to return to the same hamster wheel of the corporate world.

I also remember describing my retirement plan to Anna and saying, "That's when I can do what I really want". What? Wait 25 years to do what I really want? How ridiculous does that sound? Spend 25 years existing just to get to the point where I feel I can do what I really want.

Life is short. Twenty-five years could be a third of my life, what a waste.

That's what inspired me to throw caution to the wind and get on with things, like starting my first company, Fill That Space, although in 2020 I decided to close the company. That's what still inspires me today. Don't get me wrong, I'm not careless. I've got my eyes open. I'd never do anything to jeopardise the security of my family and my relationship. My husband is fully aware of what I want even if I can't always explain exactly what I'm doing.

I truly believe that if I hadn't met Anna and if I hadn't been brave enough to make my dreams a reality then I'd be in a very unhappy place today. I'd be waking up every morning thinking, 'here we go again'. Going to a job that paid the bills but left me feeling stifled and as if I was just a number.

Whereas today, things are so different. I love what I do. I love having the freedom that being a business owner gives me. And more importantly, I love being able to help.

I'm lucky. I was in a position where I could take that leap of faith. Make changes immediately. Without really having a plan. Over the last few years, I've learned so much and with the support of my family and friends, I'm now in a position where I actually feel like I'm living. I've taken back control, I'm now where I'm meant to be.

It's been emotional and I've had low moments. Moments where I just wanted to hide. But I've also had so many awesome moments. Moments that regularly remind me that leaving my job was the right decision.

This is going to sound like a cliché but I now feel more comfortable in my skin. I feel better mentally and physically. And for me, it all comes down to mindset. The way I talk to myself, the way I view things and being open to what could be. Being aware of my actions and reactions. And so, I can be the best I can be, one part of which is being the best mum to my kids. Not perfect, just the best I can be.

I know that I'm not alone in how I felt. You see, as mums, we're very good at putting the needs of everyone else ahead of our own. It's what we do. It's in our DNA. After all, back in the day whilst the men were out hunting, the women were looking after things. It's our default position.

That's why I now help other mums who are feeling the same. Mums who are stuck. Mums who want to make changes. Mums who just need that helping hand to take action. You see, sometimes you know something is missing but you don't know what it is. I help busy working mums find out what it is and then help them to take action, so that they can do something about it.

"Even if you are on the right track, you'll get run over if you just sit there."

Will Rodgers

MARK TANNER

Mark has recently been called 'a brilliant copywriter' by one company who speaks about how his writing 'talks to you, draws you in and engages you'.

He started writing at 11 as a hobby and is a qualified Trainer, Project Manager, Accountant, Coach and Copywriter. He has now built an agency that trains and coaches business owners on copywriting and writes for many diverse industries.

Mark also volunteers for 'The Angels of Hope', a humanitarian aid charity, that works in the remote villages of Western Kenya, and is very active in supporting global tree planting charities.

Connect with Mark:

https://www.linkedin.com/in/markhtanner/

https://www.facebook.com/mark.tanner.9279/

https://www.facebook.com/GCWContent

Day of Determination

I pulled the change from my pocket and looked at the princely total of £3.74. I knew my wallet was empty and my heart sank even further as I looked at the £6.99 price on the book for the seventh time. It screamed at me, "You see, you are a loser and can't even afford this book!"

That was not what I had just read. This book told me that I could have anything I wanted, as long as I was intentional about it. Well, I was. I was determined to buy this book but unfortunately, not today. I glanced at my watch, returned the book to the shelf and walked out of the shop and across the road to the courtroom.

The room was small, stuffy and somehow detached from reality. I was told to wait on the plastic bucket chairs that reminded me of sitting outside my old headmaster's office. I looked around at the others slumped in their chairs, heads hung, looking as morose as I was feeling. I tried to sit upright but felt the chair moulding me into a slumped position. The chair eventually won. One by one, we were called to the small counter, affording no privacy, to put our hand on the Bible and confess to our 'sin' of deciding to take bankruptcy.

"Decide?" I felt like shouting. It was hardly a decision, more of an inevitability, having been embezzled. I felt angry, defeated and now, watching all these poor souls shuffling to this small hole in the wall, powerless.

I slumped further into the unforgiving, vinyl chair. I became aware that as soon as one emptied, another victim took up occupancy. My bankruptcy papers showed I was case number 696 out of 2,541 and that was just in one month.

I was relieved as my name was eventually called. A squinty little man pointed to the Bible and commanded in a squeaky, monotonous voice for me to put my right hand on it and read from a card he thrust into my left hand. I repeated the words without any comprehension and, as I did, I noticed a sense of relief pervade through me. I was finally going to be able to sleep at night and release the constant churning stomach of the past few months.

I walked back out into the world, the sense of relief now turning into euphoria. I had just been given a blank sheet, to be able to start over afresh. Yes, I was bankrupt, had lost my business and income, but the shackles had been unchained and I could walk upright again.

I started towards the market and the river beyond, thinking about the short extract I had read earlier, asking me to seek out the values I hold most dear.

Clearly, freedom was one of them, if not the most important one. I felt free now and started to smile, something I hadn't remembered doing in years. At that moment, I felt an immense gratitude to something, I just wasn't sure what that something was.

As I reached the market, I was drawn to the smell of Indian spices. The menu, chicken madras and rice for three pounds. There were a couple of small tables free so I ordered a meal and could just afford a small bottle of water as well.

I sat down with my food and started to laugh. Here I was, sitting on a street, eating a surprisingly tasty meal out of a polystyrene tray with plastic cutlery and I felt like a king. I had a return bus ticket in my pocket and a few coppers but at least, for the moment anyway, I had a home to return to.

My brain was racing as I travelled back home on the bus. During the earlier ride into town, I had felt humiliated, ashamed and guilty of everything that had led up to what I would later call my 'day of disgust'. However, during the ride back home, I realised that this was also my 'day of determination'. I swore to myself that I would never be in this position again.

The short extract I had read from 'The Secret' that morning, contained enough wisdom for me to understand that everything was down to me. I had created this situation through my own thoughts.

I started to think about how that applied to my bankruptcy. I realised that this was the culmination of all the poor decisions I had made throughout my life. My poor decisions had come from my poor thinking.

I had been in debt ever since I was 17, when I received my first credit card. I had behaved like an excited kid in a candy shop, spending freely on dinners and booze. Even when I had a well-paid, corporate life, I had still lived beyond my means, not thinking about the consequences of my actions.

Playing one card off against another, I thought I was in control. In a final act of madness, I wrote a cheque, using my remaining credit card balance, my ego telling me how good I would look when I put the lion's share of equity into the new company. It wasn't even my money to spend but I had to satisfy my hungry ego.

My reverie was broken as the bus pulled up at my stop. As I walked along the street in the sunshine, I reflected on my oath. This was my 'day of determination'. I would never revisit this moment in my life again, as long as I was breathing.

A month later, I was reading my own copy of 'The Secret', which I devoured in a day. A month after that, I had the CD and was engrossed in it as I rode the bus into town for a job interview. I purposefully arrived early, so I could use the time to sit on a park bench, imagining myself in my job, at my desk, earning my income and loving life again.

A year later, I had my bankruptcy discharge letter and although I still had another two years to pay the bankruptcy trustee, I was now in control. Now, I had also learned to lock my ego up in a box, to stop his incessant tapping on my shoulder and clamouring for attention.

There were still hard times, of course. My crumbling marriage, a victim of my bankruptcy, was now broken and it wasn't long before I left the family home for my own mental health, let alone that of the rest of the family. Money was still very tight as my income wasn't huge but I was still managing to live debt free.

However, old habits still have a tendency of resurfacing and, as most monsters that are trapped often do, my ego found a way out of that box. He wheedled his way into my brain again and the old cycle restarted. A few credit cards here, a couple of loans there but hey, I was convinced that I could manage them, especially as I had just moved to better paid position.

I was still keeping pace with them, although the balances were inexorably increasing. Then, for a fourth time, I was made redundant. My immediate feeling was of anger and I vowed never to work for another employer again. I looked around for business opportunities, took out a start-up loan and started an Amazon business.

I never made enough profit from that to cover my monthly bills, so I started dipping into the loan to supplement my income. The vicious downward spiral was repeating and I was receding into that black hole of angst, despair and inadequacy.

Just over three years ago, I found myself almost at the place where, 15 years before, I had sworn to myself I would never be again. I felt powerless. The sleepless nights had returned and I could feel I was becoming angrier and more resentful. "How could this be happening to me again?" I kept asking. I was on the verge of giving up but then I remembered the invaluable learning that everything is down to me and my mental attitude.

I was determined that I was going to change my circumstances and set about researching how I could do that. Then one morning, as I was scrolling through the internet, I found a gem. It was another book, titled 'Paid in Full', and I was intrigued. This time, unlike the last critical moment, I could afford to buy this book. I downloaded the book and although not the quickest of readers, I completed it in a day, taking copious notes of actions to take.

The book made me realise that I had become casual about the mental work that, just as physical exercise, hones the body and needs to be worked on every day in order to create that dream life we want. The author, Sanae Floyd, offered a coaching programme which I enrolled in, which I still follow and have repeated the process from three times now. Those actions hauled me from the brink of that abyss and have changed my world completely.

So where am I now?

I now have a viable business, doing what I love, which is constantly growing and contributing to others through my writing and coaching. I am now living with my soulmate, whom I will soon marry and I am able to regularly contribute to various charities that are close to my heart.

The lessons I have learned along this tortuous journey have been invaluable and I now read every day, to grow my awareness and my skills. I believe in a higher power that guides, advises and protects me and is always available to support me.

I have been asked many times about the steps that brought me here.

The first is to understand your own values and beliefs. Not those of others that you may have adopted from childhood onwards but those that really resonate with you and that you can claim as your own.

Secondly, learn how to master and quieten your ego. My ego is full of its own pride, that believes that it doesn't need any help from anyone else. It has led me into many disastrous situations, but now I am aware and in control, it no longer does. Your ego may have a different character, so take the time to understand it.

Thirdly, keep living your dream in your mind. Spend the time to envision you living in that world where your goals and desires have already been achieved. Create that vision board and spend time in front of it every day, living in the moments that you have created.

Fourth, create an unshakeable belief that a force greater than you is by your side. Universal Energy, Master Intelligence, God, your Higher Self, whatever you call it is your choice, but just know there is something greater than ourselves, of which we are part, that works for us and brings us opportunities we can never imagine, as long as we look for them.

Fifth, take the action you need toward your goals, every day. For years, I was amassing wisdom and knowledge but I was only putting a small amount of that into action. Knowledge is useless without action and it is by doing that we create our wisdom. Everything is created in thought first but it is only when that thought is acted upon that we create that physical reality.

Finally, be grateful and happy for all you have. There are always millions who are less fortunate than you, whether that be physically, mentally or financially. Take the time every day to give thanks for at least 10 things you have, however small they may be. Giving sincere thanks will put you into a happy state and when we are happy, magical things happen.

"The real test is not whether you avoid this failure, because you won't. It's whether you let it harden or shame you into inaction, or whether you learn from it; whether you choose to persevere."

Barack Obama

MARLA SAGGU

Marla Saggu is the founder of Marla Investments, an Entrepreneur and an Investor. She has been on a journey through two continents and many different industries and bought and sold a few businesses in the last 15 years, each time exiting after growth and a substantial increase in the value of the business.

She now acquires businesses that are looking to exit but don't like the normal process of selling a company. She works with owners, making their needs and their emotional value integral and crucial to the selling process so that they can leave a legacy while maximising their return.

A Business Story: My Journey

I have had a lot of conversations with business owners where we have talked about our business journeys and how they have led us to where we are today. Most of the conversations have been with women and despite being successful in their fields, they would not have imagined they would be where they are today. Their own journeys were supposedly destined to end with more modest outcomes and so they put on their imposter syndrome overcoat and carried it around with them.

A lot has been written on imposter syndrome and I am not trying to give any advice on that particular subject matter. I am not really qualified as I have not quite managed to throw that overcoat away myself. It creeps in just like a well-loved but tattered piece of clothing that we just don't want to send to the incinerator that it belongs in.

What interested me were the journeys all these women had been on. I am not saying that it is any different for men but my reference points have come from my discussions with women. It got me thinking about my journey and how I would have never imagined that I would be here. If at 17 you had told me that I would be the Managing Director of a £21 million turnover business, had bought and sold many other businesses along the way and was now heading my own acquisition arm, I would have said that you were dreaming. At 17, I was still negotiating being allowed to go to university.

I grew up as the eldest of three in a fairly traditional Sikh extended family of 11 in Kenya. My father was a successful businessman, a pillar of his community and very well known in the then small town of Nairobi. Trying to have some individuality and independence in an environment where the collective was more important than any one person was challenging, especially as I was destined to have an arranged marriage by the time I was 18. Paradoxically, my father was very keen that I received a good education and attain fantastic results en route to this marriage—a heavy burden!

When I was 13, like a typical teenager, I was fighting to be my own person in the most discreet way possible. The repercussions for being overtly rebellious were too severe to even consider throwing any tantrums or raising my voice. So I decided that my identity was never going to be attached to any man's surname. In my very small way, I determined that my signature would only ever be my first name and one day I would be my own master in charge of my own destiny. It would not be changed because I got married and one day people would recognise me solely by my first name. My signature has developed but not changed much since I was 13.

My father taught me my first valuable business skill; negotiation. The expectation was that I would do my A levels and a suitable boy would be found for me to marry. It took a year of carefully planting the seeds and then watering the tiny sprouts from a wavering mind, for him to agree to let me go to university. As long as it was a three-year course that had a nine to five job at the end of it and I came home and got married immediately afterwards. It was a start and it got me out of marriage at 18.

However, he also made sure that I had all the necessary skills to be a 'good wife'. I was taught to cook, sew, crochet, knit, embroider and make sure the household ran seamlessly, so when I did eventually get married at 30, I was well equipped to be a 1970s housewife.

I studied optometry in Manchester. We were called Ophthalmic Opticians in those days and paid quite well for our expertise. It wasn't a job I was mentally or emotionally suited to. There are only so many times you can say, "better with or without", "clearer on the red or the green", or "better with one or two or the same" before it loses its charm. I also hated being stuck in a dark room all day, especially in winter. What I did enjoy was talking to our patients and styling them, so they went out of the door looking fantastic in their glasses. I liked people and still do and that for me seemed to be the only positive aspect.

At 22 I had taken the then very bold and uncertain step of becoming a locum in an age where everyone was looking for stable, lifelong employment. I loved the freedom of working in different environments and working with different people and more importantly, for me, the freedom to choose where and who I worked for. In essence, running my own one-woman show. My biggest learning at this time was how successful practices were always run with a vision and genuine caring for the staff. These were practices where all the staff thought about how they could provide the best service for their customers while keeping their focus on sales. They understood their well-being was a direct result of the well-being of their business. Conversely, there were just as many scraping through with disengaged and uninterested employees.

My true business journey started with me opening my first practice. That is where I realised that I enjoyed running and growing a business much more than being in a dark room all day. I liked the interaction with customers and staff, talking and negotiating with suppliers and finding solutions to problems. I enjoyed offering the best customer service and seeing smiles when the spectacles someone had chosen were not only visually correct but made them feel stylish. The whole process of overseeing the direction of a business was enlightening and exciting. My decisions and how I reacted to problems made a difference to bottom line profits and growth. I watched my staff thrive and grow with mentoring and training, and the loyalty and love from the staff will stay with me always.

When I sold that business, I was ready for a break and thought that the life of a lady of leisure was just what I needed. It bored me to death and I was soon running a baking business from home. However, I am not the domestic kind and I either had to scale up or close up. So I became a Consultant Optometrist, working with other retailers to help them improve their offering. This was a hard lesson because you discover that changes can only be brought about if you are open to them and do not let your ego get in the way. If someone does not want to listen to your advice then you are wasting your time and energy. Walk away.

The skills I learnt over those 24 years formed the basis of all my other ventures, whether it was running a food business, consultancy work or running fuel forecourts. What I learnt was that it didn't really matter what the business was, the foundations of all successful businesses have the same building blocks and principles. You can learn the nuts and bolts of an industry, you can learn all the technical details, you can even learn to operate machinery, but if you don't have the basics right then it is an uphill battle.

So, what do you need to do as a business leader?

You need strategic focus, but this is just one of the elements of good governance leaders need to succeed. You also need to have values and beliefs to guide effective decision-making; the right culture in place to get engagement from your own people and other stakeholders; processes and procedures governing things like operations and communication; having the right people in the right roles and developing others to reach their full potential. Last but not least, you need the right checks and balances to ensure the good financial health of your company.

I remember being terrified the day before I took over as Managing Director of KSC Worldwide. What did I know about running fuel forecourts? I had decided that I would watch and listen for the first month before I started changing things. This wonderful sentiment lasted a week and whilst I realised that I may not know a lot about bunkering and how a veeder root worked, I did know when a business was in slow decline and needed a sharp kick up the backside. I knew that I had to take the helm of this big ship immediately if it was going to avoid the iceberg. The funny thing was that on 1st July 2014, when I took over the role, I didn't know that I knew how to do this. I only knew that I needed a management team that were empowered and skilled in their own areas and the buy-in from my workforce.

My focus has always been people. No matter what business you are in, I think that there is always one golden rule; your business grows or fails by how valued every single person in that business feels. We had no money to invest, very poor staff morale and no management team. So I did what was to me the most important thing of all—talk to as many people as I could away from the office or any of the sites.

I discovered that we employed some fantastic loyal people who had no direction or purpose. Everyone had been taught to view each other as rivals not team members and they were fiercely self-protective. We got every single member of staff to write on two different coloured Post-it Notes; one was what they loved or wanted to love about their work and the other was what they hated or did not want to face when they went to work. I still have a large envelope full of those Post-it Notes and those thoughts formed our values booklet. This was written in plain English and every member of staff signed it happily because they could see their own words there. It changed the culture of our company and started a shoestring growth in revenue, customer service and loyalty that I could not have foreseen.

Six and a half years later, with substantial growth in the meantime, I was concentrating mainly on strategising instead of operational problems. We had an amazing management team who understood and implemented our values and beliefs to create a culture of 'can do'. Every member of staff knew their purpose; they knew how they personally contributed to the well-being of the business and themselves and they knew they mattered. We sold the business this February and it was the most emotional week for all of us, there were lots and lots of tears. We had increased the business value but it was also difficult to let go.

I can truly say that I have appreciated every moment of my business life—the good and the bad. My journey has not been a straight line but it has been educational and enlightening. I learnt what was valuable in business but I also learnt how to value myself and my knowledge. Accepting that I don't know everything and never will but I can learn how to do things better by opening my mind and asking for advice was hugely edifying. But you have to leave your ego at home and listen properly and allow people a voice. You may not implement what is being said but ignoring or failing to acknowledge or appreciate an opinion does not allow an organisation to unite behind your goal.

Most of all I enjoyed it and made my own road to success. Everyone has a unique quality—we can all shine in our own way.

"Forget past mistakes. Forget failures. Forget everything except what you're going to do now and do it."

William Durant

NICKY MARSHALL

Nicky is an award-winning, international Speaker and best-selling Author. She is also a mum, nan and wife and loves nothing more than family time.

At 40, Nicky suffered and recovered from a disabling stroke - inspiring a life's mission to make a bigger difference.

Nicky has an accountancy background and 20 years of helping people improve their health and wellbeing under her belt. Combining both, Nicky is a Mentor, seasoned Workplace Facilitator and Keynote Speaker, inspiring people to discover their own brand of Bounce! Nicky's knowledge, knack for stressbusting, hugs and infectious laugh make her an in demand and popular speaker.

With passion in buckets and a penchant for keeping it simple, Nicky has a unique talent in breaking down the barriers that hold people back from living a life they love.

Be careful if you stand too close—her enthusiasm rubs off!

Follow these links to connect with Nicky:

www.discoveryourbounce.com

www.facebook.com/discoveryourbounce

www.twitter.com/dyblifestyle

https://www.youtube.com/channel/UCBXK2Ut7IyL39-Pc1cRr2lA

Or send her an e-mail: nicky@discoveryourbounce.com

To view Nicky's books: https://authorcentral.amazon.co.uk/gp/books

A Passion Can Flourish If You Feed It

I started writing for fun when I was 10. My mum helped me write a poem for a 'Keep Britain Tidy' competition and I loved it. Mum has wonderful handwriting, which even looks artistic, and she had a love for books and knowledge, so I guess this rubbed off a little.

I was good at English at school and when I chose to do accountancy training it was always my written skills that shone…the maths took a little more effort! As my first marriage was coming to an end, I embarked on a more spiritual journey and wrote meditations under a full moon. I would have a line or two in my head for a couple of days, usually as a result of a scene in nature or a scenario in life. Once I had put the girls to bed the rest seemed to flow, as if it came from somewhere else; a stream of consciousness if you like.

As my personal status changed so did my job title. After many years in accounts, I retrained in a variety of holistic therapies and my enthusiasm for helping and supporting others became a vocation. I also started to teach, something I never thought I would have the confidence for. I taught Reiki and Tarot and wrote my own courses, not knowing that my writing CV was ever-growing.

Alongside these career changes my spiritual journey developed further. I found my own happiness through bold action, reflection and a ton of self-enquiry. When I met Phil, my second husband, I remember him saying, "Wow, you make life so complicated!" He said it in jest, but he had a point. I had got to a stage in my life where I didn't just put up with how life was—if it wasn't making me happy, I would change it.

As I started to experience just what was possible, it seemed a natural progression to want to inspire others. I started public speaking, nervously, to small groups and was encouraged to send a few articles to magazines. After three were published in the same month I had my answer: I could write content that people wanted to read and share!

As well as a writer, I was a realist. Through my personal development I had a shelf full of books and had met many inspirational people. Those that were successful in a writing career mostly used their book as one stream of revenue, alongside paid speaking events and courses. This suited me fine. I yearned to speak on bigger stages; the nerves were still there but better controlled and I thrived when working on multiple projects.

My holistic therapies were changing too. As well as the actual therapies I was giving more advice about self-care for the times in between appointments. This developed more and more until The Bounce

Programme—a six-part mentoring programme—was launched in 2013 as part of my new company, Discover Your Bounce.

By this time, I had self-published two books. One was a collection of the inspiration that had continued to flow since my meditation writing, the other was a fictional story with its plot based on my life experiences. In 2010 I had also suffered and consequently recovered from a life-changing stroke, which led to Rescued By The Coastguard being launched in 2016. This book was 'the one'. The one that took soul searching, lots of tears and many realisations. The one that was hard to finish—I had a two-year gap where I was unable to work out how to finish the book and I wondered if it would ever see the light of day. A dive in the Isles of Scilly turned out to be what I needed, the last three chapters flowed the next day and voilà!

I had also contributed chapters to several other books; on motherhood, confidence, forgiveness, business and the law of attraction. Life experiences can be great subject matter! At the time I was having fun writing and contributing, but all along my confidence and skills were growing.

In 2017 a lovely friend and mentoring client called Lynn mentioned that she had always wanted to get her book published. I started giving her a few tips and a bit of advice, after which she asked me if I would publish her book. After an initial no and a long ponder I thought, 'why not?'

Lynn knew this was the first book I had published beside my own and we learned the process together. I already had the team and knew all the elements, but this felt different somehow; it felt ok to be experimenting with my own words, but looking after someone else's work was a new level of responsibility!

While my writing and publishing journey was bubbling along, my other business had been growing and by this point I had a new venture and a new business partner, Sharon.

Sharon had started helping as a Non-Executive Director in Discover Your Bounce and together we launched Discover Your Bounce For Business, offering corporate wellbeing workshops and events. As we both came from a corporate background this felt like the next logical step and our personalities meant not only did we have a real laugh, we also very quickly created a new brand and customer base.

So when Lynn's book, Trailblazing the Way from Victim to Victor, was launched in May 2018, we had a realisation: we had another business!

Discover Your Bounce Publishing has grown so much since that day. We have a great production team and not only give book advice, but with our business backgrounds can also advise an author on how to use their book as part of their wider business. Having over 35 years' experience of being business owners between us, we can also help with sourcing branding, PR and marketing, the book launch itself and that imposter syndrome that almost always rears its head.

I've made a few realisations along the way. Firstly, if you actually get your book to print you are way ahead of the crowd. So many people I speak to say they have an idea for a book or a manuscript half written. To take the next steps to publishing takes dogged determination, as the editing process can feel like it will never end. It also takes confidence building and being open to the opinions of others (the right person will be objective but encouraging). Finally, you need to feel the very real fear that no one will buy it, or people will hate it, and do it anyway! You may ask yourself, 'Who am I to write about this?' but I would counter, 'If not you, then who?'

Only you can explain that business concept or write that piece of inspiration your way. You may have an experience, or view, or way of expressing yourself that really engages and helps people. You could inspire someone to take an amazing and daring step in their own life…or maybe just to sleep at night. However you influence someone, the fact is that if you don't complete and publish your book you just won't and the opportunity will be lost.

Through every article published, every blog, every chapter and every book I have realised that what I think and write has value to someone. I know I have changed the direction of a person's life through my words and that is really special.

By feeding my passion I have enabled it to flourish. I have honed my craft, learned new skills. I have had failures, crises of confidence and bounce backs. I now take pride in every word. I love that through publishing I can enable others to find and share their own unique voice. In doing so, many change their life for the better along the way.

So if today you are reading this book and you have the tiniest gossamer thread of an idea, I would encourage you to feed it your energy, to love and to nurture it and one day it too will flourish.

"Imagination is everything. It is the preview of life's coming attractions."

Albert Einstein

QUENTIN CROWE

Quentin Crowe is an award-winning marketer and educator. He is the founder of QCx Consulting and currently the Chief Learning Officer at White Marble Marketing.

His mission is to help senior managers suffering from various forms of *imposter syndrome* unleash their hidden potential. He provides 1:1 support, mastermind groups and training courses using his 'Power of PEERs' approach.

Over the last 20 years Quentin has trained more than 5,000 marketers around the world including more unusual locations such as Albania, Bulgaria, Nigeria and Vietnam.

His book *The Marketing Imposter* will be published in July 2021.

Learn more about and connect with Quentin:

https://www.quentincrowe.org

https://www.twitter.com/QtheMarketer

Taking a Cold Shower

Feeling the Heat

A forlorn figure trudges across Kennington Park in south London. Oblivious to the summer sun on his back, his mind is in turmoil. He knows that life will never be the same again.

He has spent the morning analysing bank statements and spreadsheets. After 14 years of trading, the horrible reality hits home. His business is insolvent. Worse still, the cashflow forecasts suggest the position will only deteriorate.

The following months are a blur of dispiriting activity.

He tries to cash in his pension to generate funds, but not yet 55, he is too young to be eligible. Swallowing his pride, he approaches competitors who, sensing weakness, crawl over the numbers with glee. They don't want to buy. They know there will soon be a carcass to pick over.

After three months of manic activity, suddenly all is quiet. The business is dead and with it his livelihood and reputation.

When a business fails, it hurts. It hurts suppliers, employees, customers, shareholders and associated loved ones. When some of the suppliers are sole traders, those unpaid invoices have significant consequences— cancelled holidays, shelved plans and unfulfilled promises. When employees have trusted their futures in the business, they now have the painful process of finding new jobs. And when shareholders are also family and friends, the pain and embarrassment is acute for all concerned.

Hurt can lead to anger and anger craves a focus. That focus, quite understandably, was me. It was me who had let so many people down and I certainly felt the heat of that anger.

The nadir—a few weeks after the business collapse, I bumped into an old colleague in the street. He cut me dead. I can still feel the burning hatred in his eyes as he turned and walked away from me. To many (but not all), I was a pariah and they cut their ties with me.

Embracing the Cold

As the founder and leader of a business, my ego enjoyed the status of being the boss. People deferred to me, laughed at my jokes, regardless of how unfunny they were. They sought my attention and my approval. Like so many ego-centric leaders, I believed these people respected me the person, rather than the power I represented. When my business failed, that power evaporated along with much of my reputation.

Thankfully, I had some positives in my life which ensured I did not become too self-obsessed and depressed.

In contrast to the vitriol that had been directed at me, there were others who were incredibly supportive; notably those who had also lost businesses. They would regularly check in with me, offering support, advice and guidance.

More humbling still, was a former employee who was more concerned for me losing my business than her losing her job.

And most importantly my wife, who despite her disappointment and pain, continued to love and support me. In late summer, our daughter was to be married. We knew that despite everything, her wedding would be the abiding memory of that year. And so, it has proven.

Rebuilding Process

But the immediate reality was that our finances were dire. What savings we had were gone and my credit cards were almost maxed out. I needed to swallow my pride and earn some money—sharpish.

But how? I was over 50, I had not been in the job market for more than 15 years, so who would employ me?

Step One - **Drink a lot of coffee**.

Plundering my network, I set up 'catch-up coffees' with as many people as would meet with me. Seeking their advice was invaluable. I eked out some coaching work, work which only six months ago I would not have considered. But coaching proved both rewarding and cathartic. Two of these clients even paid me up front. Their generosity was a financial lifeline. Other opportunities started to emerge, which turned into small projects and progressed to longer-term contracts.

I had turned the corner and survived. Now it was time to be more strategic. After all, time ticks mercilessly by and there were still the significant issues of a mortgage to pay off and long-term financial security. I had always assumed that my business would see me through to retirement and its sale would be our pension pot. That plan was in tatters. I was financially worse off than at any other time since my twenties. This wasn't how it was supposed to be. It was no good feeling sorry for myself, I needed a new approach for what was left of my career.

Step Two – **Re-evaluation**.

Without the daily burden of a business to run, I now had both the time and energy to think, research and plan. I embarked on a voyage of self-discovery, exploring the work of the ancient and modern, from Enneagrams to 10x thinking, from Marcus Aurelius to Jay Shetti. I also sought the opinions of others. Their feedback was both humbling and inspiring. All of which enabled me to take a cold, hard look at my strengths and weaknesses.

On the positive side, I learned that my primary attribute is as a guide. People told me that they valued my skills as a trainer, coach and mentor. This insight helped me clarify my purpose—to help people and organisations unleash their hidden potential. By aligning my purpose and skills to what might be of value to others, I found clarity.

I also confronted my weaknesses head on. I recognised that at my worst, I can lack focus and am easily distracted. So, I have learned a range of new techniques to help me build on my strengths and constrain my weaknesses. I listed those techniques that appealed most and converted them into checklists. My daily checklists included journaling, meditation and cold showers. But checklists are little more than good intentions. And as my grandfather used to remind me: the road to hell is paved with good intentions. In other words, intention is worse than nothing without action. To turn my life around, that action needed to be consistent, or in other words, a habit.

Step Three – **Build new habits.**

There are of course good and bad habits. Bad habits compromise short-term gain for long-term loss. In the moment ice cream is highly enjoyable, but in the longer-term, the fat and sugar of ice cream is detrimental to health. Good habits conversely compromise short-term loss for longer-term gain. Enter cold showers.

By chance, I came across Wim Hoff and his extraordinary cold water exploits. I thought I would give cold showers a go, not realising how transformative this simple habit would become. I started slow. Having enjoyed a normal hot shower, I turned the thermostat from hot to cold, just for one second. Gradually I increased the duration to 30 seconds. Washing off conditioner became my trigger to the turning of the thermostat from hot to cold.

I tracked the habit. Once I had consistently achieved six days out of seven for three months, cold showers were engrained as a habit. Oddly, I now find it impossible to have a shower without turning the thermostat from hot to cold! It has become an integral part of my daily routine.

After each cold shower, my body responds by radiating warmth. I have clarity and energy to take on the day ahead.

Enjoying the Warm Glow

I look back and barely recognize my former self. Having spent 14 years operating in an insular market, my outlook was so blinkered. I was both bored and no doubt boring.

Freed from the shackles of my old business, those blinkers have been removed. My days look so different now. I have found work in the most unexpected and rewarding places including charities, multinationals, agencies, SMEs and start-ups. Each new client has provided me with fascinating new insights and perspectives. And as for those creditors who did stay in contact, I have found opportunities to pass work their way, slowly repaying my debt to them.

New habits are helping me to be more productive. The more productive I become, the more energy I have and the more ambitious my thinking becomes. During this time, I have learned that I have so much more to offer as a result of my chastening experiences. I have had the privilege of creating training and coaching programmes for entrepreneurs and senior marketers also suffering from various forms of imposter syndrome. We now have a growing alumni community of like-minded individuals, each keen to unleash their hidden potential. We meet up in the form of mastermind groups, using the collective intelligence of the group to solve individual member challenges.

So, each morning my cold shower has become so much more than a just a habit. It acts as a metaphor and a catalyst for my new life.

I enjoy the hot water but recognise that too much time basking in the heat will lead to complacency. I am reminded of my past. When I turn the thermostat from hot to cold, I have learned to welcome that initial shock. The shock reminds me of my current reality. And as I get out of the shower, I am glowing with energy, excited for the day ahead and my longer-term future.

I would never have believed it that summer's day in Kennington Park, but my business failing was the best thing that could have happened to me.

"Character cannot be developed in ease and quiet. Only through experience of trial and suffering can the soul be strengthened, ambition inspired and success achieved."

Helen Keller

RUPA DATTA

Rupa is a recovering recruiter who realised very early on the importance of relationships. She spent the second phase of her career in mobile workforce solutions holding roles in sales, customer experience and project management. She is passionate about the future of work and the place portfolio careers play in that world.

In addition to helping others through Portfolio People, her own current portfolio includes pairing sparkling wine and Indian food and growing a property networking organisation. She holds an MBA from Henley Business School and in 2020, became the youngest ever female to join the Toastmasters International UK Leadership Team.

Connect with Rupa and learn more about what she does:

Email: rupa@portfolio-people.com

https://www.twitter.com/Rupa_Datta00

https://www.portfolio-people.com

Why Grief Is an Inevitable Part of Your Career Game – and How You Can Embrace it

At the time of writing this chapter, we had experienced a global shift and reset that touched almost everybody. Whilst economic crises and wars indeed have an economic and political ripple effect for years, and even decades, after, the global pandemic that was Covid-19 was more obvious with all generations impacted. With loss also comes opportunity and 2020 gave us all the chance to take stock of what we have been doing with our lives, and, inevitably, what we wish to do moving forward. Navigating our careers forms part of that.

For my own generation, borderline Gen X and Gen Y (depending on who you ask), and for the generations before and after, we were conditioned to have a 'hold a job for life' mentality. Land a role, work hard and you will be rewarded by higher pay or promotion. This has no doubt changed however expectations and the concept of security can be deeply rooted in one's psyche, largely borne out of the stability required by our parents, grandparents and great grandparents, based on their experiences.

Let's Go Back in Time...

I think it is important for all of us to understand, where possible, where we have come from in order to chart where we are and where we will go. I'll take myself as an example, looking back on four decades of life.

Born in 1980, I'm the eldest of two children to first generation Indian immigrants to England. Both sides of my family were directly impacted by the partition of India in 1947. I can only imagine what that must have felt like, however that scale of displacement will no doubt highlight the need for security. Emigrating to another country also lends itself to regeneration and a need for stability.

To make a sweeping generalisation as a result of these experiences, perhaps most of the second generation kids of that time were raised with a strong work ethic. I certainly was and whilst that may not have manifested itself in certain role expectations, it comes across in all that I do. There is a melting pot of influences here and exploring all of them could be a book in itself. Both of my parents were ultimately career civil servants and luckily they enjoyed their jobs. I can't help but wonder what paths they would have taken had more choice been available to them, and what both my brother and I were and were unable to do also as a result.

Before we move on, let me invite you to take a moment to reflect on your influences.

Phase One - Falling into a Career or Perfectly Planned?

If environment plays a part in career decision making, then another familial influence may be what sectors, industries and job types you are exposed to. The oversimplified version of this for my family would be academia or business. My brother went in one direction and I in the other. I used to joke that he knew his career plan 20 years ahead of time (and probably still does!), whereas I didn't know what I was doing the next day. That has of course changed over time and we are probably both somewhere closer to the middle of the spectrum these days.

I started paid work as soon as I was able. In hindsight, this was a combination of work ethic, and a desire to have my own money or perhaps a sense of financial freedom at that stage of my life. These were largely customer facing roles to begin with that undoubtedly had an influence on what would be my later career path. I recall also being a favourite of a temp agency or two, saying yes to most things if I was available.

This continued throughout university and for a couple of years post-graduation. Eventually, I fell into the world of recruitment where I stayed with the same company for seven years. I attribute the longevity of this stint, and that it was in the same company, to my boss/mentor at the time. Someone that took a chance on me, created opportunities for development and kept the variety alive through change and stretch assignments. I may not have realised it then but knowledge and experience that I gained during that period would certainly stand me in good stead a few years later.

The seven-year itch is called that for a reason. The time eventually came to move on. Although this was largely by choice, there was a sense of loss involved, which is only natural when something has been wrapped up in your identity for so long.

Checkpoint: What did your early career look like? Write down any key reflections.

If you are still in the early part of your career, is your role giving you a good basis for your future? Are you dabbling before specialising?

Phase Two - Breaking Free or Free Falling?

My initial intention was to undertake an MBA concurrently whilst in the aforementioned role. For one reason or another it didn't play out that way.

It worked out for the best, I believe. I had some form of structure to follow in the form of post-graduate education, yet a bit of time and space to take stock, reflect, breathe and perhaps even grieve. It took me another three years to realise it and define it but it was from this point on that I truly started to build a portfolio career.

Falling into self-employment within a year simply by asking someone I had met a few months earlier if they needed help with a problem that they had described to me, I was able to generate revenue as a result and started to build a small consultancy through referrals. In this time, I'd also started an events business on the back of a napkin with two friends that we shut after only a few months.

Again, completely by accident, I also embarked on what would become my volunteering/not-for-profit career. Something that will always have a place now that I have discovered it. It has spanned the charity sector, social enterprise and a global not-for-profit. An example of where you can give your skills and keep them sharp.

Checkpoint: Do you do different types of 'work'? Do you volunteer? Are you studying something? If the answer is yes, you may well be starting to build a portfolio. If the answer is no, take a moment to reflect on whether you would like to.

Phase Three - So What Is a Portfolio Career (and Common Misconceptions)?

The term goes back to the work of Charles Handy. The oversimplified version is that there are different types of work in life that he had placed into four categories: paid, home, gift and study. Over the last few decades this has been adapted. We may commonly hear it synonymous with the 'gig economy' or 'side hustles.' Personally, I think this is a dilution of what is great about how a portfolio career can all come together and has an adverse effect on a true portfolio person to be taken seriously.

Another misconception is that you have a portfolio career if you have left corporate life and are self-employed or freelance and thus potentially working for different clients. Whilst there is a high proportion of people in this category, you can comfortably have a portfolio career whilst holding a full-time job. In fact, an overwhelming desire to untangle the labels associated with independent working became my final research project whilst at business school.

Robert Kiyosaki's ESBI matrix charts the path of someone moving from employment to investor from a financial perspective. I can't help but wonder if there is a synergy between this and the route to building a portfolio career from a time perspective. I've been fortunate enough to see more and better opportunities present themselves as a result of taking this route and being open to the process. Sowing seeds is easy, patience for the seeds to bear fruit is quite another thing.

Checkpoint: Do you sow seeds of opportunity for yourself? Do you let these seeds germinate? Might you have too little or too many?

Phase Four - If the Future of Work Is Truly Flexible, Is a Portfolio Career the Answer?

Over the last decade, I returned to the corporate world for about three years. I managed to sustain my portfolio career during that period, all that changed was where I had to focus my attention and energies. Since leaving that role, I found my 'gift' and 'study' work to be a constant though the latter has advanced a little.

I put to you that this past year we've all addressed what 'home' is and means to us. For some people this may have been uncomfortable. For some it may be an assessment of how our situation can or cannot contribute to the basis for a portfolio career. One of my lockdown wins is cooking more, and a happy result of this has been pairing sparkling wine with Indian food and being regularly featured in www.glassofbubbly.com

As we move into the next normal, some companies are super charging the way on results based, remote working. Others are arguably hanging on to the past. How and where we work continues to evolve and with that comes the opportunity to be more open-minded about what can be done within the hours of nine to five for example, companies embracing new ways of working and development opportunities within this time. Within a business, this could mean keeping people longer for the right reasons. If you are developing a portfolio outside of this, however, you are more likely to have blurred lines between paid work and other types of work. This need not be a negative thing, but an awareness of this and how to manage it is indeed important.

Where Do We Go From Here?

Change or any sort of transition in life involves a period of grief. Sometimes it is obvious or expected. Other times it is the loss of a habit or the familiar. Whether you make a conscious decision to change job/career/role or it happens to you that feeling is the same. Perhaps we have been given the opportunity to build a career and a life outside of the framework given to us. Something that we were designed to do and that existed beforehand.

While a period of mourning may exist with every change I've experienced as a portfolio person, knowing that there are other parts of my portfolio that act as a constant in any given time becomes that necessary security. Better still, the magic that happens when the strands all come together is pretty powerful. I invite you to try it, because we're all portfolio now.

"Success is not the key to happiness. Happiness is the key to success. If you love what you are doing, you will be successful."

Albert Schweitzer

SHARON CRITCHLOW

Sharon is an international best-selling Writer, Conference Speaker and Vocal Changemaker. She brings passion to the subjects of the future of work, wellbeing, diversity, emotional intelligence and environmental social governance.

Sharon is a qualified Accountant with over 20 years of experience in senior leadership roles and growing successful businesses. Within Discover Your Bounce, Sharon is a Presenter and Facilitator, she also looks after the finances and provides strategic direction for the group. A qualified Coach and Mentor, Sharon is passionate about people becoming the best that they can be and allowing their true talents to shine.

In her spare time Sharon is an advocate for the Association of Chartered Certified Accountants (ACCA) encouraging people in to the profession and supporting their development. She also enjoys music and has been known to play the flute and sing—although not at the same time!

Email: Sharon@discoveryourbounce.com

https://www.discoveryourbounce.com

https://www.linkedin.com/in/sharoncritchlow

https://www.twitter.com/sharoncritchlow

The Business Of People

In 2020 we were shown that things change. Sometimes you work towards a goal and change is gradual and feels under our control, whilst other times change happens overnight and you have no power to determine what will happen next. Interestingly, rapid change is not always bad; good fortune and a change in direction can also come in a flash.

My story starts in a cafe in Torquay, not sipping a cappuccino but making the cappuccinos for other people. I would look across the harbour at the yachts and that carefree life was what I wanted. School had been a bit of a disaster and higher education was not possible. Fortune led me into accountancy and an open access way of learning. I was so grateful to have that chance to make up time and have a different life. What was even better is that the problem solver in me loved that there was a correct answer.

I soon came to learn that much depended upon circumstances and this nuanced the position. The more senior I became, the more I understood that interpretation, intention and risk also played a part in finding the right answer. These are all discerned by people, not textbooks. This science of right and wrong that I had found could sometimes be more of an art, and so it is with life. We can walk a clear path that seemingly suits us, but challenges along the way enable our judgement to be involved. Whilst the original path may have all the right characteristics, as it changes direction we may realise this suits us more...even if it was not what we imagined.

My career hasn't grown in the way I imagined it would in 1990. I thought I would be in public practice as an accountant forever. However, alongside my love of numbers and business grew a fascination with people. If people influence business, what influences people? It would be many years before this aspect of my thinking was truly explored.

I had qualified as an accountant really quickly and my practical experience to date did not match my level of education. I moved jobs upon qualifying and I struggled to teach myself parts of the new job. Any mistakes came with a harsh reproach and no support to improve.

After nearly eight years as a public practice accountant, I felt trapped. My team were fab, but my boss undermined me and failed to help me when I asked. Part of the issue was that I challenged the status quo about the services we offered, all well-intentioned but not well received! On my last day he told me he was pleased I was leaving as I posed a threat to his influence over the business. I had tried to move companies, but there were few jobs around and, reluctantly, I left that town and the career I thought I would always have in search of something else.

The problem was I knew the attitude my boss held was not unusual and I didn't feel emotionally strong enough to walk in to a similar situation again. For the first time I looked at the qualifications I had slaved over and thought, 'How else can I use what I have?' I was offered an interview at a financial services business and the team looked fun.

I had worked within the financial services regulatory framework before so it came easily to me and what I brought to this new situation was operational process, regulatory foresight and horizon scanning. How could we prepare ourselves for what is coming our way? What is the world saying and what can we put in place now? Taking these big concepts and making them into an action plan was what I did best. I differentiated us as a brand through aligning with Investors in People status and Corporate Chartered membership. My role soon became a board position and we grew the company in a multimillion-pound business.

Exit Stage Left

Then I started being undermined by my peers for a second time and it became clear that our values were no longer aligned. I made a brave move; despite being a shareholding director, I left and took stock of my options. That in itself is quite an eye opener. One day I was a director, the next I was…?

People often ask you what you do and I didn't have an answer. Now, 25 years into a commercial career, I had to ask myself, 'What am I good at? What really interests me?' In all of my previous jobs I had encouraged others and supported their work progression. I loved to support people to strive for success and then relax into a role and make it their own. A series of poor managers had made me aware of what makes a team thrive and how much time can be wasted when decisions are made without a productive outcome in mind. My active management had launched careers and opened doors to progression for others. Now it was time to do the same for myself.

Whilst I was exhausted and burned out, again, this time my recovery was swift and I put my horizon scanning head back on to see what the world needed and that I could offer solutions for. That was 2016 and by the end of the year my world would look very different.

A Realisation

I had been an Operations and Compliance Director with some financial advisory clients of my own for most of my career. I looked at the cards and emails of support and thanks I had received from clients and staff on leaving the business after 17 years and something occurred to me. Here were cards saying thank you for my patience, for making people feel empowered, for listening. I thought I was selling financial services solutions, but no one thanked me for my taxation planning or for getting their pensions organised. It turns out what they were buying wasn't what I thought I was selling!

It was time to re-evaluate what I really offer to the world. I asked a few people their thoughts on my position and the feedback was that I was a natural coach and mentor. I explored this a bit further and was the only non-Learning and Development person on my master's level coaching course. I loved it and discovered that many of the techniques I had used to support others had names! Who knew? It was great to fill in the gaps in my knowledge and to explore what else was out there.

Bouncing Back

2016 passed in a blur. The loss of two family members and the realisation that a third needed care took time and energy, but I was glad I had that to give. I was also asked by Nicky Marshall to be her Non-Executive Director in Discover Your Bounce, which is a personal development business. I wondered what people would think of the choices I had made. It turned out that those who had worked for me said it was very me.

The first shock was when Nicky asked me to help her at a talk to 90 people at a bank. I took the microphone and did my bit. I was nervous, but I had felt this before. As a Regional Chair at Association of Chartered Certified Accountants (ACCA) I had to introduce speakers at our evening events and the first time I did it I was physically shaking. This time it was much better and more speaking events found their way into my diary. I now enjoy public speaking both on stage and online. It gives me the opportunity to challenge everyone to look at the world around them and their place in it.

My commercial experience of a regulatory background and a personal development interest has now formed a new career. My big picture and trend spotting capabilities have found a home. I facilitate groups and deliver workshops which tackle human workplace challenges and help individuals and teams to thrive. I coach and mentor executives and I write; this was one of my biggest shockers! I have gone from struggling to read and write at school to being published in magazines and online around well-being topics. Furthermore, in 2018 a publishing business emerged from Discover Your Bounce, so now there are other authors we support on their journey too.

Imposter Syndrome

It was also suggested that I put myself forward to stand for Council at ACCA and in September 2016, much to my surprise, I was duly elected. I felt like a fraud. Here were proper accountants doing important jobs in big businesses, and here was me, coaching and speaking at businesses about mental health. One day a Council colleague very kindly said that there were things they could learn from me when it comes to people and performance. I eventually found my place on the Regulatory Board at ACCA, using my nearly 20 years of experience to best effect. I also got involved with supporting initiatives around emotional intelligence and leading inclusion, all things that sit well with my personal development experience.

The Common Thread

Accountant, Financial Planner, Operations and Compliance Director, Writer, Speaker and Coach. You could be excused for wondering where the common thread is. For me, it is people. I used to explain to new Financial Advisers that the value of a pension was not just money; it represented all of the times that person had missed their child's school play, all of the work calls taken on holiday and the sleepless nights. My opening words when I teach accountants at the start of their leadership career is to remember that accountancy is a people business. Everything you produce has an impact on people. It can bring about redundancies, it decides if shareholders have a dividend, it allows new jobs to be created.

Thinking back, there have been a few common themes in my career. Valuing, supporting and promoting others, spotting what is needed in the world and taking action and giving a new dimension of myself some space to grow. It has taken me from accountancy to the commercial world, to a global role at ACCA and to being a writer, speaker and coach. Everything I have seen and done moulds the things I write and speak about and, far from feeling like an imposter, I have now embraced who I am and what I bring to the world.

Finding Your Passion

Here are a few thoughts for anyone looking to change direction:

- Find yourself. Take a look at the things you do well and the things you are passionate about. Often others can spot your underlying talents and it is not unusual to think that everyone has the skills you have, but no one else is you. Whatever it is, you can put your stamp on it and do it your way. To quote a famous song, '*It ain't what you do, it's the way that you do it, that's what gets results.*'

- Find your tribe. Who can you learn from? Who will challenge you and who will support you to explore your talents? Allow yourself space to grow and remember that your development is your responsibility alone.

- Create a clear vision of what you want. Easier said than done? Sometimes a clear intention is all that is needed so that you can spot new opportunities. Use journaling and reflection to enable you to discern between opportunities and ask if it is you or not you. Eventually, a clearer vision will emerge.

- It's never too late to shine.

"Many of life's failures are people who did not realize how close they were to success when they gave up."

Thomas Edison

TAMZIN BRAIN

Tamzin is a Hypno-counsellor with over 10 years of experience running her private therapy practice, which she successfully built up alongside a full-time job in secondary education. She is passionate about helping people to recognise their full potential and to step into their awesomeness.

Tamzin works with adults and children, 1:1 and in groups. She offers mental health and wellbeing workshops and therapy programmes designed to support clients in losing weight, stress management, childbirth, etc. She also teaches meditation and mindfulness and even offers past-life regression sessions.

Alongside her business, she is busy looking after her children and walking her therapy dog, she has also been known to jump out of planes, drive supercars, sing, dance and write poetry.

Contact and connect with Tamzin:

Email: hypnochange4u@gmail.com

https://tamzinbrain-evans.tribesites.com/
https://www.hypnochange4u.co.uk/

https://www.linkedin.com/in/tamzin-brain-evans-ab716044/

https://www.twitter.com/hypnochange4u

https://www.facebook.com/HypnoChange4U

Phone Number: 07919990804

Fear and Hope

I would like to dedicate this chapter to my Mum, Vada Brain, who supported me so much in just about everything, walking with me and cheering me on as I built my business from the seed to the tree it has become. She too was a self-employed therapist and very successful: she helped many people and touched many lives. She was my inspiration and my biggest fan, and I wish she were here to see my next achievement, within the pages of this chapter. I know she would be so proud.

My Journey...

The journey to my career started when I was just 13 years old, when I was a 'teenage counsellor' to my friends as we navigated our teenage years together. I added official qualifications to my compassionate nature, my natural interest in people and good set of communication skills. After graduating with a degree in Psychology and Criminology, I then took a five-year detour through the forests of sales and marketing and spent over 10 years exploring working in education. Whilst also raising two children, building on my own education, developing new skills and slowly making my way back to find myself and my next direction. In this chapter I hope to share some of this journey with you, in particular my transition from full-time employment to full-time self-employment.

What Did You Do?

I moved from the security and stability of employment to the uncertainty and unpredictability of self-employment.

How Did It Feel?

It felt scary and stressful but also exciting, I felt brave doing it and stepping outside my comfort zone.

Why Did You Do It?

It was a combination of factors, there was a part of me that was tired and frustrated by the limitations of employment: I wanted so much to use my skills and I was so tired of having to prove the value and the worth of the work I did. I felt like my desire to help children to the best of my abilities, was falling on deaf ears. I wanted to apply the wide range of skills I had to improve the children's coping skills and enhance their future life

I could see the benefit and value of the content that I was teaching so clearly, but felt like no one else could, nor did they appreciate what I did. It was very infuriating. Not to mention the fact that I felt so restricted, like a bird born to fly, but being kept in a cage with their wings clipped. I felt I could benefit more people and be appreciated more by working for myself.

Why Do You Do It?

I love the work I do. When I work with my clients, the look on their face and the way they seem so much lighter after their hypnotherapy session is priceless. Or when I can see the personal and emotional shifts my clients make, after a course of counselling with me, I know that I am doing the best I can to help as many people as I can.

Why Didn't You Do It Straightaway?

The main thing that held me back from becoming self-employed full-time sooner was fear and hope: I feared failure and worried I wouldn't be able to earn enough to keep up my financial contribution to the household bills, which was necessary.

At the time my husband could not have paid all our bills by himself. I did not have the luxury and safety of being financially comfortable, or secure, whilst I explored, or even played at, being a business owner, like when you're a child and you get to play shopkeeper. I felt we could not have afforded for my business not to work. Now I am in a more comfortable place with the business, but more importantly I am more confident and braver too. Having made these internal shifts, I am able to reflect more logically and see some of the alternatives, should my business have not succeeded. Alternatives that are sometimes hard to see when your judgment is clouded by fear and lack of confidence.

The other thing I mentioned was hope: there was a part of me that held back from making the shift sooner because of hope. I hoped my full-time employment would open more doors, I hoped that they would one day see the value of the work I was doing. I hoped all my spreadsheets, data collection and feedback (which my kind Dad, Phil Brain, also helped me with and worked tirelessly on) would be taken on board and add measurable value. Add something quantifiable, that could prove to the powers that be and the purse strings that the work I did was a worthwhile investment, that it helped many students to develop lifelong, transferable skills.

I hoped I was a resource worth utilising for the benefit of many more children. Something that an Investor In People school could understand the value of. Whilst this may come across as quite negative, what I hope to convey is merely the feelings of frustration I experienced at the time of my transition to full-time business owner. I also hope to highlight how, not only did changing from being employed to being self-employed involve a literal, physical change, but it also involved a mindset shift. I needed to build my confidence and self-belief. I also had to trust myself and the world enough to know that, if I created the space for self-employment to be part of my life, then it would become part of my life and I would succeed.

Why Did You Stay in Employment for the Time That You Did?

I stayed in employment for as long as I did because of the fear I mentioned. But I also felt I needed to align myself properly before taking the final leap, a leap that I had struggled to make by myself. In fact, had it not been for the fact that I was made redundant, combined with the incredible support and patience from my wonderful husband, Nigel Evans, and our incredible children, Delano and Tiona, I may still not have made the leap when I did, which was five years ago.

There were some other factors that had kept me there too; consistent, predictable income and a pension, a lovely team and financial and personal security.

What Was Good and Bad About Moving to Self-Employment?

There are many things that are good about moving to self-employment and some challenges to self-employment too. What I really appreciate about being self-employed is that I can decide what rates I want to charge, how to organise my time and when to schedule appointments. It works perfectly around my family and gives me more time with my two lovely children.

However, it's not always easy juggling running a business as well as taking care of myself and my family. It can be very stressful and difficult to create and stick to clear boundaries, especially as I work from home. But it is rewarding and working from home has a number of benefits too. Apart from saving money on business premises rates, I can use the time that would have been spent travelling to and from a therapy room or rooms in other ways and it means I can be a great deal more flexible with my time.

I can make it fit around my family, instead of having to fit my family in around it. I can go to all Delano and Tiona's sports days, shows, fairs, cake sales and parent's evenings. I can be as involved in the school community as I want to be, if I want to be and give something that way too. I have a choice. I can create more time for Nigel and I, we can take a drive out in the country for a spot of lunch or have brunch in a local café after morning drop off.

I also realise the greatest value for me in being self-employed is more about the time it creates, than the money. After the bills are paid and our basic needs met, I can put as much or as little work into it as I want to and in theory make as much money as I want. As long as there are always people who believe they are worth investing in and so are willing to pay for the services I offer.

What Have You Learned?

Being self-employed there is a massive amount of learning to do, it is a huge learning curve, like I had never experienced before. Running a business, I have had to multiply my skill set 10-fold. I have had to learn about tax, self-assessment, accounts, private pensions and start using spreadsheets in new ways and for new purposes. I have had to learn about how to set up, develop and design my website. Also, how to use several social media platforms for marketing purposes, events, adverts, promoting my business, networking and interacting with different kinds of people. I have had to develop and promote face to face and online events and workshops; liaise with other schools and businesses and learn how to use a variety of new software and apps. I have also had to develop different communication skills. Whilst I have had several years of experience in selling products, learning to sell myself and my skills involves utilising a whole new set of people skills; the list is endless.

Overall, I have learned it helps to be flexible, open-minded and creative; to be brave and bold and step out of my comfort zone. I have learned to be experimental and not to be afraid to try different things, different tacks and different approaches.

My mum offered words of encouragement when she reminded me that it is also important to trust the process. To understand that sometimes things happen for a reason and as a consequence they create space to allow more positive things to follow. For example, when I was made redundant, at first it was a shock that I had not seen coming, I felt confused, angry, and unappreciated. The redundancy confirmed my feelings of being undervalued in that environment. I also felt sad, as it meant I would no longer see my wonderful colleagues or be part of that incredible team. There was some relief and reassurance that I was not the only one facing redundancy but I felt sad for everyone else and worried about myself and them. What would happen now, what would we do and would we all be okay?

However, there was a part of me that trusted things would be okay and regarded the redundancy as a blessing in disguise. It would give me the kick, the motivation and the drive that I needed to allow myself to embrace the opportunity this presented. To fully commit to my business and my needs in a way that would enable me to push some of my internally created boundaries, expand and start the journey towards my professional development and personal growth. I am not there yet, but for me there is so much value in the journey and the experiences I am exposed to and open myself up to.

The other blessing redundancy gave me was the opportunity to take a very special trip with my, then six-year-old, daughter to see family in Australia, some of whom she would be meeting for the first time. Being able to share this experience with her was very special and has created some precious memories for us both. It was also the last time I got to see my granny, who despite the physical distance, I feel very close to. Our creativity, open-mindedness, willingness to try new things and shared spirit of adventure connected us and I see some of that in my amazing daughter too, which brings me feelings of such joy and pride.

First Day of Self-Employment: What Did It Feel Like?

It is hard for me to remember exactly what my first day of being fully self-employed felt like, but I imaginember* (*when you are not sure if something is a memory or your imagination) I likely felt relaxed and excited that I could go at my own pace and allow my creativity to brim forth and flow.

Being self-employed comes with a barrage or responsibility, steep learning curves and a wide range of feelings. For me, no two days are the same, this is partly due to my poor organisational skills, which presents a massive challenge in itself. But also because of the uncertainty of it all, combined with the events that are unfolding in my internal and external worlds.

There are good days, when I feel I am fully in control, focused, determined, motivated, driven, clear thinking and right on track, like a train without detours. Then there are the other days when I feel more like a slow boat on a meandering river, distracted by anything and everything, being pulled this way and that, indecisive, foggy-headed and sluggish. Then there are the rapids, where everything is happening so fast around me that it makes my head spin. I feel overwhelmed, confused, scatty and all over the place and (please forgive the expression) lose my shit!

The other place I sometimes find myself in is inertia, sometimes it is hard to stop and change direction and sometimes it is hard to get going. At these times I have to remind myself to be kind to myself, take stock, re-group, re-energise and enjoy the stillness, or the ride, created by these natural states of being. I can use this time to prepare myself for the next part of the journey.

Self-employment allows me the opportunity to master my own destiny and design my life the way I want it to be. There can be a lot of movement and with it, perpetual change and growth. In the words of Ronan Keating, "Life is a rollercoaster, just gotta ride it".

What Are Your Biggest Success Points?

Hello… I'm running my own business.

In all seriousness, how does 88 clients in six months sound, alongside working two and a half days a week and raising a family (a one- and a three-year-old)? In January 2012, I decided to run a (Groupon/marketing) promotion, where I sold 88 discount hypnotherapy vouchers. These vouchers offered between one and four sessions to the purchaser, so that's between 88 and 352 hypnotherapy appointments! Or how about starting three years of diplomas just four days after having your second baby, she even came to one of my training days, curled up in a sling at just a few weeks old.

These are two of my biggest success points, but every day I feel I make small successes. Whilst they do not represent enormous, immediate, financial success, they contributed towards my financial potential and my personal growth. They helped me build a lot of confidence in my abilities. The fierce determination I showed helped me know that I was on the right path and reassured me that I had made the right choices. I did and still do experience parental guilt, which is when I have to remind myself to be kind to myself and it helps me reaffirm, reassert and redefine my boundaries.

Becoming self-employed is one of the most challenging, exciting, scary, freeing, stressful and limitless things you can do. But it is a decision I am very happy to have made and one that allows me to fully step into my own.

"I feel that luck is preparation meeting opportunity."

Oprah Winfrey

THOMAS BASSETT

Tom is a father, husband and lover of physical activity who has taken part in many different disciplines over the years. He believes that being physically active is more powerful than we have yet to fully understand.

Contact Tom:

Phone: 07773302935

Email: allaspectfitness@gmail.com

Know Thy Heart

Just before my first child was born, we found ourselves in a situation that was not ideal. My wife has an amazing job as an engineer. She did some calculations as we were looking at maternity pay and we found out that the loss of her main income was going to massively affect our lifestyle. During those months prior to our firstborn son's arrival, we made a decision that I would try and grow my business. At that time I did not achieve this, unfortunately, due to lack of knowledge and lack of support in business development. I had failed.

One week before my son was born I got a job as a school caretaker in a prestigious Bristol School. As School Caretaker, I would unlock the school at 6:30am every weekday and I would finish at 2:30pm. However, I did not go straight home after work, due to some success in building my fitness business. I had several personal trainer (PT) clients as well as running group circuit training sessions. Finishing work at 2:30pm, I then started work for my own business at 3p.m. This meant most days of the week I would not be home until around 8 or 9pm. My wife, looking after our first child, was left alone from 5am to whatever time I got home at night. This stress put pressure on my family, it was exhausting emotionally, financially and spiritually.

After a few short weeks it became apparent my wife was not coping. I came home one day from work to find the house empty and my wife and my three-month child gone. I got a text, she was going to her parents for a while to have a rest. My heart sank, I had failed in business, I had failed in work, I had failed as a family man providing the most basic of needs.

This for me was the lowest point I can think of to actually reach.

Ahead of my son's christening, around his first birthday, surrounded by family and friends, I organised a pub meal not far from the church, for myself and my brothers and sisters. We planned to meet for a family meal, the first one we would have had in a very long time, all the kids were there, my brothers and sisters, and my dad. We were meant to meet at about 6pm. The table was all booked. Unfortunately, my family are bad timekeepers. They were late. My dad is not in good health and doesn't really do anything very quickly. As my smiling older sister walked through the pub door she greeted me with the normal hug… but I couldn't let go. I buried my face in her shoulder and sobbed, I don't remember ever crying that hard. She physically held me up while holding me tightly, her little brother crying his eyes out. This small detail about my brothers and sisters being a bit late for a family meal was enough to tip me over the edge. In the middle of a pub in Devon. I broke down and cried like I have never cried before.

I was exhausted. I was getting worse and worse, I felt that my wife and I would slowly slip down a dark path. My route was a little bit darker than hers. I had started to drink, not just one or two bottles a week, more like three or four a night. It became apparent I was developing a bit of a drinking problem. One morning, while at work, dealing with all the different things, never seeing any progress, never seeing money in the bank, all I saw was my belly expanding. My waistline folding over my jeans whilst I tried to teach others to be fit and healthy. For me the contrast between what I saw and felt and what I was known for was too much. I found some beer in a back store in the school and opened the bottle at 9am.

After this, my wife and I had a long conversation, many of you might think I would just stop, slow down, forgiving all to fail again, but I couldn't do that, I wouldn't do that. We made the decision that I would leave my full-time paid job, for the next year we built up our savings. I went completely self-employed, for the first time, nearly 10 months after that decision. I took a few weeks out to settle into my new way of life. This was September 2019, I was now living my dream job teaching people to be fit, strong, healthy and well. 1 spent a few weeks getting my fitness back up to standard, losing weight and feeling better. I stopped drinking, I started running again, I started weight training again, I joined the kettlebell club to give me some focus and I started my own fitness park in Filton, Bristol. With this huge lifestyle change we went into 2020 with our hearts full of hope and joy. However, life and the universe had a big curveball. Just as my season was due to start in March 2020, Covid-19 arrived, this was a big, ugly and depressing change. Suddenly, I found myself in my worst-case scenario. My business relied on people paying me to go to a gym to teach them to be healthier and stronger; to help them lose weight and reach their goals. The gyms were all shut.

We were in lockdown!

So what do you do? You've just found yourself sliding down a very very steep mountain, bouncing off every single rock on the way down with absolutely no control over where you're going to land and what you're going to do... Well unfortunately for some people, people I knew, they stopped, they grabbed onto whatever they could and they stopped their businesses, they shut their doors. They did not want to change, they blamed the situation, they blamed others, they blamed the government, their customers at the gyms, they even blamed the conspiracy theorists. And me; what did I do well? I've already hit rock bottom. I'd already hit my face on the soul of my stomach. There was no lower for me to go, the only way I was going was back up the massive bloody mountain. I looked at my now two-year-old son and my beautiful wife. I looked at myself in the mirror and I said to myself now is the time to change, now is the time to grow. I started doing online training for the first time ever. Online was completely alien to me, I had no idea if my training style would work, I had no idea if anybody would turn up, but I stuck with it. Some sessions I might get one person, some I'd get 10. I signed up with online companies to help build my business and advertise myself properly. I have no knowledge of how to build a business in the physical world. I had to rely completely on instinct and knowing that the bottom of the mountain is not where I want to be. My wife was still working, she was doing 12 hour days three days a week to support what was happening with the government, furloughs and company contracts. I was with our two-year-old son everyday all day. It was exhausting trying to do online training, generate new business, come up with new ideas, get ahead of the curve and be the father of a two-year-old who just wanted a cuddle. While I was teaching online, I trained, I worked my arse off to make sure I brought some money in. The money slowly started coming in, a couple of £100 here and there. I got some cash in hand work doing odd jobs cutting grass, trimming trees and working for farmers moving bales of hay. I took anything I could get my hands on to keep the bills paid. Never letting it compromise my business, my passion. In October 2020, I had a small blessing, I had got a part-time weekend job. I did not go down the route of getting a full-time job, mostly because I was working so hard on building my fitness business that it was starting to make some money, enough to buy food and fuel, I was starting to achieve.

It is when we suffer the most that we find out what we are made of. We can all live in our comfort zone, whilst life around us keeps moving on. We avoid our problems and shelter from the storms, but never adapt. It's the times when we feel the lowest that we become our strongest.

Who Am I?

My name is Thomas Bassett. I am a Physical Training Instructor. I love my life and I love my work. I now have a successful online fitness company. I have multiple private clients and I'm the manager of an outdoor training facility in Bristol. I am fitter and stronger and more resilient than I can remember. I am the proud father of two amazing children. I have an incredible bond with my son Arnold. When he was born, I didn't actually see him properly for nearly a year, despite only sleeping 10 feet away from him. Whilst following my passion and gathering support, over the last few years, I have grown closer to my son and my wife. I have a wonderful loving relationship, and most of all I actually get to spend quality time with my newborn baby daughter. I do not miss a moment with them. I will never again sacrifice myself to the perceived societal norms. I will teach my children to follow their passions and dreams. This does not mean I will protect them from failure. I will let them fail. I will let them learn for themselves what their passion is. We can only guide the people around us, they must first choose their direction.

"It's in times when we struggle the most, that our potential is brought out of us, when we follow our passion."

Thomas Bassett

"I never dreamed about success. I worked for it."

Estée Lauder

TRACEY MCCARTHY

Tracey is an HR Consultant specialising in the not-for-profit sectors. Her business, HR Services Bristol, began in 2012 and continues to go from strength to strength.

In addition to her career, Tracey has had many voluntary roles over the last 22 years, including Chair of Governors, Charity Trustee and Appropriate Adult.

She lives with her husband in South Gloucestershire. Her family and her voluntary work leave little time to focus on household chores—just how she likes it!

Connect with Tracey:

https://www.hrservicesbristol.co.uk

https://www.twittiner.com/hrservbristol

https://www.linkedin.com/in/hrservicesbristol

https://www.facebook.com/HRServicesBristol

I Wasn't Expecting That!

You will never pass any exams! You will never get a job! So said one of my teachers, loudly and assertively in 1978. I grew up in Kingswood, near Bristol and I left school at 16, with a handful of mediocre grades from the exams I sat. Despite high levels of unemployment, I was fortunate in securing a permanent job within months. I worked as an Administrator for the next 11 years, in a number of different departments for the John Lewis Partnership in central Bristol. I married at 22 and had the first of my two daughters when I was 28.

Fast-forward to 1999, shortly before the lunar eclipse.

"Are you sitting down?" Words you don't want to hear from a family member on the telephone.

My 57-year-old dad had died of a heart attack earlier that day. He was found in bed by his widowed mother, who he had been visiting at her home in Padstow. He was an only child, my mum and dad had divorced 12 years earlier; my grandfather had died in a car accident a few months before I was born. I was now next-of-kin for my 84-year-old grandmother. I could not imagine what she was going through.

At the same time, my mother-in-law had recently been diagnosed with dementia and lived on her own. She lived near to us in Bristol and had no other family members she could call on for support apart from her son and his family.

I had been working as a Credit Controller for an accountancy firm in Clifton, Bristol for a few years. Pressure was on me, as you would expect, to collect outstanding debts from clients. However, whatever I achieved never seemed to be enough and I became aware that the future looked bleak for the company. My concerns were well founded, as they went into liquidation six weeks after I left them.

I was married with two daughters at primary school. I was rather busy at the end of the last century!

I found the voluntary role of governor at Barton Hill Infant and Nursery School in Bristol rewarding. When the opportunity for paid work in the same community became available, I was immediately interested. With imminent redundancy a reality, the timing was ideal. It was a part-time role, not far from home, which would work well with a young family. I was delighted to be offered a role with Community at Heart. With a five-year, £50 million grant from the Government's New Deal for Communities initiative, it was an exciting time to be part of a regeneration programme for parts of inner-city East Bristol.

The job description for my new role was vague to say the least! "What will I be doing?" I asked my line manager, Angela Bragg. "I'm not sure, but we need to recruit staff urgently," she replied. Right there, in that moment, my HR career started.

I had clicked with Angela straight away. We have lots in common, including our work ethic and ability to bounce back from significant challenges (most of the time!). Angela was keen to develop all those in her team to be the best they could be. She would often say, "I'm training Tracey up for my job."

Angela supported me to gain the knowledge, skills and experience to progress in the HR profession. This included arranging for me to have a mentor; an HR Manager in the public sector, securing funding for training and planning exposure to experiences to cement my knowledge. She was (and still is) an inspirational woman. I remember telling her that I had been elected vice chair of the governing body of Barton Hill Infant and Nursery School. "Why aren't you the chair?!" she exclaimed. "There isn't a vacancy for that role," I replied. "Oh, I suppose that is a good reason." Angela is now a dear friend and my life has been better for having her in it.

Working at Community at Heart was the best job I'd ever had. The organisation's values and mine were so similar, and I believed the regeneration programmes would make a significant difference for thousands of people. This experience has enabled me to focus on what I feel passionate about: supporting charities, community groups and social enterprises to deliver to often the most vulnerable in society. Community at Heart summed it up!

Meeting Angela was life changing for me. Angela had experienced similar issues to those I was facing, in her past. She often said that whatever was happening in her life, her career was her constant, something that she had full control of and gave her strength.

Whilst not a formal training programme, the structure Angela had in place for everyone in her team was empowering. Everyone was encouraged to reach their potential. This included mentoring (both internal and external), which was invaluable.

After an intensive two years in post, I started work on obtaining a degree level qualification in management. Having never enjoyed academic study, particularly exams, I couldn't believe how much I enjoyed it. I would get up at 5am to get everything ready for the day ahead and settling down to college work before I woke my daughters up for school. I would then do the school run, go into the office for six hours, school run again and then start the family evening routine. Work was quite demanding at this time, as we were set challenging targets by central government. Added to this, we were committed to the involvement of the residents that we were providing services to at every level, this often led to highly charged, stressful situations!

Angela ensured I had a firm foundation for my HR career, coaching me to get as much experience as possible. This included having a set of keys thrown at me by an employee who had been caught not working her hours each week, who promptly walked out!

I realised just how much experience I had gained when I was working for a large charity shortly after leaving Community at Heart. The head of the organisation said she wanted the most senior HR advisor on a particular case. I looked at my colleague, who had recently completed a postgraduate qualification in HR management (and I had not). It was me she wanted, as I had greater experience of advising on and managing complex issues.

Twenty years on, after the management qualification, I achieved an HR management qualification. I have worked in a variety of sectors, including the NHS, manufacturing, retail and social care. In 2012 I decided to start my own business, so that I could focus on delivering the best pragmatic advice and customer care.

I specialise in the sectors where I started my career: voluntary groups, charities and social enterprises. We used to call these the not-for-profits. I wake up every day looking forward to getting to work supporting leaders in organisations to be the best employers they can be. I always aim to be a trusted partner for any client I work with.

Focusing on a new career, which I love, gave me enormous strength to cope with the personal issues I faced leading up to the end of the last century.

If I were to give my younger self some advice it would be; don't listen to what everyone tells you (especially that teacher!), the best is yet to come.

"The best investment is in the tools of one's own trade."

Benjamin Franklin

ZOE KNIGHT

Zoe Knight is a professional Life and Business Coach working with creative business owners to bring energy and joy back into their business. Zoe's top core value is freedom and she strongly believes that we should be free to live the life we want, the way we want. Her work is helping and inspiring others to achieve this through her coaching, mentoring and speaking.

Other than enjoying her work with her clients she also loves embracing the glorious countryside and all that nature has to offer. She spends much time exploring walks in the stunning village where she lives with her beautiful boys.

Connect with Zoe:

https://www.zoeknightcoaching.co.uk

https://www.linkedin.com/in/zoeknightcoaching/

https://www.instagram.com/zoe.knight.coaching/

https://www.facebook.com/zoeknightcoaching

From Doubt to Determination

When you need to explain who you are, you begin to wonder, where do I start? My birthdate and birthplace? My favourite food? My favourite teddy as a child? The big events in my life which undoubtedly helped shape who I am today? There are so many options—but I shall stay general for now. My name is Zoe, I had a wonderful childhood (though I could certainly paint a darker picture of it if I chose to view it that way). My mum was unconventional and wonderfully supportive and that is what I remember the most. She instilled in me a belief that I could and should do whatever I wanted to do and be whoever I wanted to be. What an incredible gift to give a child and now I have two children of my own, I hope I can do the same for them.

Embracing My Passions

So, for the most part that is what I did. I wanted to be an actress so I studied performing arts at college. Despite other people's concerns that I was 'putting all my eggs in one basket' it never occurred to me not to, or that I should consider anything else. I then left college and my country, aged 17 and went travelling around the world with an open ticket and no set plans. Again, nothing other than visions of what adventures lay ahead and going where the wind would take me. Two years later I returned with plans of freedom, more travels, being a waitress, auditions and getting a break to start my acting career. But, as often happens, that is not what life had planned for me. I met a man and fell in love. Head over heels deeply in love. I didn't want to do the long-distance relationship thing and he was very settled, so I changed course. If it wasn't acting it was going to be animals! I had a deep passion for animal welfare and so I went into that. Despite a good education, I was happiest hands on and getting dirty doing the practical work. I had worked hands on with Vervet Monkeys at a rehabilitation centre in South Africa so back home I went to work for a horse sanctuary. As part of the horse care team and then as an animal welfare assistant, I gave practical care to a wide variety of animals at the college. I earned minimum wage and worked long hours but I was immensely happy.

Life seemed pretty perfect on paper. Married at 23, bought a house at 24, first child at 25, second child at 27, but behind the scenes something wasn't right. A shift had happened. As much as I thought and expected to be a natural earth mother, I suffered badly with post-natal depression. As the lower earner I had to compromise on my jobs. Starting at 7.30 in the morning doesn't work well with childcare and so I found a part-time job working for a conservation charity. This was conservation as opposed to welfare, but I could get behind the organisation, which was important to me. After a couple of years I moved to another charity job that I could get behind. However, they were part-time office roles because that is what worked around my young children. As much as I loved who I worked for, I knew that I was not made for an office desk job. It was sucking the joy from me.

Searching for What Was Right for Me

As I searched and clutched at other ideas, for a job that I would enjoy, to do more training in something that would inspire me, I was met with (not my own!) concerns. Concerns that I wouldn't do it, that self-employment was a risk and that learning a new skill, if I didn't see it through, was a waste of time and money. I took these fears and concerns on as my own and so I stayed in my role, unhappy, unfulfilled and desperate to find something that would relight my fire, spark my joy and ignite my passion. At the same time my husband and I grew further and further apart. I tried to ignore the horrible unpleasant feelings for years but eventually I had to face them. I was unhappy. We were unhappy. We had so much love but for some reason nothing was changing, despite counselling, and it seemed that our journey had come to an end. My world was shattered. I wanted to be with that man forever. He was all I had known for my entire adult life since I was 19. I didn't want to break up a family. How would my children cope? It wasn't just us, but our families too, they had been a huge part of our lives for 14 years. The guilt. The concerns. How would I cope as a single mum? Pay the bills, etc.

However, at the same time a whole world of possibilities opened up to me. Yes, the life that I had planned out was no longer on the cards, but that meant that I could go in whatever direction I wanted. I was in control. In the driving seat of my own life. What I found was that without the need to consider other people's opinions, without taking on other people's fears I had more clarity than ever about what I wanted to do. I had considered going into coaching for many years. I had always been 'that' person—you know the one. The one that all your friends come to for advice or just to be listened to. I loved people. However, I had always been talked out of it. Well, the month my husband and I decided to separate was the month that I went to London to do my first course in coaching and I have never looked back!

New Beginnings

I now have my own coaching business which is growing and growing. For anyone that wants to start their own business or start a new career, whilst juggling lots of balls and spinning lots of other plates, let me share with you my journey over the last three years, from then to now and how I managed to make it work!

After the course in London, I decided to get myself a proper qualification. I did research and had conversations to see what might suit me best and give me what I needed. I found a course that was one day a week at university, over nine months, plus working from home. At the time I was working four days a week for my charity job so I asked them if I could swap my day off each month so I could attend university. They agreed. I called in favours for childcare, to drop them off and pick them up on that day. I became obsessed. I did a huge amount of my own reading and researching. I absolutely loved it and knew it was something that I wanted to do, but when it came to the end of the course, I had my fresh qualification—then what?

Growing my confidence

I knew that to build my confidence I needed to get lots of coaching experience under my belt. It was the practice that I needed, not more reading—you can read as much as you like but if you don't take action then you won't make any progress. So, I coached. And coached. I joined lots of online groups and offered free coaching. I offered to help people. For the most part, these were online coaching sessions working with people all over the world. If I was working with someone in America or Australia it meant that I could do more because of the time difference. I would get my children to bed and then start coaching at 10 or 11 at night. I was going to do whatever it took and seize any opportunity to make it work around my very busy life of looking after my children, working four days a week and running the house, as well as the usual life admin, maintaining friendships and keeping up with family. It was exhausting, but I didn't care, because I loved it.

Money!

It got to a point where I knew what I was offering was of value, so I needed to start charging for my sessions. Enter money mindset issues, imposter syndrome, self-doubt, you name it! It took me a while and some real work on money mindset to be okay with that. If you remember, I had come from working for charities and pretty much minimum wage roles most of my life. When you do something because you love it, then it feels wrong to charge for it. I continued to do some free coaching and discounted coaching, but I did my own work and came to terms with money because if I wanted to make this work, which I did, if I wanted to do this full time so I could reach more people, then I needed to earn money from it. A business is not a business if there is no income!

The other thing I needed was time! I had one day a week for coaching, plus evenings and every other weekend, but that wasn't ideal, so I negotiated with my boss to go down to three days a week at work. I extended the hours so that I wasn't losing too much of the day job income, but it freed up an extra day to dedicate to my coaching. I was hoping to attend networking events and get myself out there as a coach! Hurrah! This was to start in March 2020 and we all know what happened then—hello lockdown! Hello home schooling. Goodbye any free time I thought I had! However, this wasn't going to stop me. We can all be immensely resourceful when we want something (the key is in finding that thing that you want that much!) and so I had to make it work. Luckily, due to working with people overseas, I was already quite used to giving sessions online over Zoom. My first paid client came during lockdown and I have grown it from there.

What Is Your 'Why'?

Anything is possible, you just need to want it enough. My advice for anyone curious about, or wanting to start a business is to make sure you know why you want it. Knowing your why will make you keep going when you don't want to. When you feel it is hard and you want to give up, when challenges arise, when you are putting yourself out there and getting nothing back. If you can tap into why you are doing it that will be your fuel to find a way. To keep pushing forward and showing up, to keep learning something new, to make new connections and ask for help, to think of alternative ways that you WILL make it work.

For me the hardest part was the marketing side of business. I like people. That is the bit I loved, working with and helping others. I couldn't care less about marketing. But I had to learn to embrace it, because I could be the best coach in the world, but if I wasn't being visible and people didn't know I existed then I wouldn't have any clients. It takes time, there will be compromise, but it starts by taking action. One small step after the other in the right direction, and soon you will look back when you are questioning what the hell you are doing and see just how far you have come.

EXPERT TOP TIPS

#1. *Tracey McCarthy, HR Services Bristol*

1. Personal development is everything – take responsibility for yours for the rest of your life!
2. Volunteering is a great way to develop knowledge and skills to support your career ambitions, especially if your paid work is not able to offer those opportunities.
3. Find out what resources are available in your area, or online, to support your development.

#2. *Tonia Galati, TG Consulting Limited, employability expert. Winner of NUE awards 2021 for social mobility projects*

1. Just go with your gut – if it feels right then it usually is, and if it doesn't feel right then it probably isn't. Life is way too short to be stuck in a role where you feel unfulfilled and unhappy.
2. Take the risk and make the change. The feeling you get when you are in a job or career that you love is indescribable. It's true when they say that if you do something you love you will never work a day in your life again.
3. Whenever I speak to people who have finally made the decision to move jobs or set up their own business, they always say 'I wish I had done it sooner'. Look at it this way – what is the worst thing that can happen? If you don't try then you will never know.

#3. *Victoria Chidgey, Director, Atoll HR*

Changing Careers:

1. Understand your values – what is important to you in life and find a company who share the same or similar values
2. Know that your career may change many times throughout your life and each new path will bring you additional skills and experience

3. Around 70% of vacancies are not advertised – it's all about utilising your network – so get out there and assess who you know and how you can benefit from your connections.

Choosing a New Career:

1. Consider your values, strengths and vocational interests when shortlisting your career options – the best job will be one that you love and have some skill or potential in.
2. Remember people change careers multiple times so have a career plan with a variety of milestones and options, just like a development plan.
3. If at first you don't succeed, try and try and try and try and try again – persistence pays off. Never give up and believe in yourself. Seek help from experts who can help you sell yourself and achieve your goals.

#4. *Tony Stubbs, CEO, Transpire, The Global Director Network*

Top Tips for those wanting to start a non-executive director career are:-

1. Being a NED is a vocation NOT a job – "Serving on a board is a responsibility & a privilege. the high points are very high, the low points properly chastening!" – Sir John Tusa. Treat yourself to some career planning advice for this next phase of your life/career to understand why you want to make this move and how it fits with other career/life goals
2. The NED market is highly competitive and very hard to break into – if you're serious, be prepared to invest time & money to work out what YOUR NED offer looks like and how to take that offer to market. Also be prepared to be resilient in the face of the inevitable rejections
3. Build up/join an appropriate network to support your new venture, that way you'll find yourself writing your own job description and you'll have a peer group to talk to – it can be a lonely life as a NED!

#5. *Rosie Skinner, Director, Mployable Consulting*

1. Treat your new job search like a job in itself. Do your research on the industry - know it inside and out, keeping up to date with the latest news and trends.
2. Network. Know the movers and shakers of your chosen industry, and reach out to them on platforms such as LinkedIn. So many positions never actually reach the job boards, because of networking and being in the right place at the right time.
3. Get the basics right. It's an obvious one, but your CV needs to be spelling and grammar checked, relevant, tidy and up to date. Ideally no more than 2 pages long, and if you've had a long or varied career offer to provide details of anything more than 10 years ago 'on request'. Unless instructed not to, a well written, tailored and interesting covering letter or note, could be the collateral that sets your application apart from the rest.

#6. *Ihqlak Hussain, Director at AMCI Associates and Author of Succeed!*

Tips for those that are seeking self-employment as a career to achieve financial freedom:

1. Dream big
   Articulate YOUR vision by initially asking the question WHY? This is to be followed by producing a mission statement and goals using SMART approach.

2. Believe
   Believe in yourself by understanding your own strengths and weaknesses. Undertake a personality test available in SUCCEED! – an inspirational toolkit for the serious entrepreneur. This will help you to evaluate your own current skill set before embarking on this incredible journey to realise your dreams.

3. Develop a business plan for your business venture.
   Do your homework (thoroughly research your business proposition). Read SUCCEED! as it provides a step by step guidance on developing a business plan that has been followed

by thousands of entrepreneurs since 2003 with 98% success rate.

#7. *Andy Weeks, Business Consultant at GetSet for Growth (YTKO Group)*

Tips to changing career:

1. What are you good at? Reflect on your key skills & competencies.
   Identify whether your top 3, match those needed in possible new role.
2. Use a sounding board: talk to other people, both inside & outside your network.
3. Don't drift: set a date to act.

Tips to choosing a new career:

1. Make a shortlist: what do I enjoy doing? What have I considered doing in the past?
2. Research: find out as much as you can & decide.
3. Get ready: what do I need to apply? How can I display myself in the best light?

ABOUT DISCOVER YOUR BOUNCE!

Discover Your Bounce has emerged as a group of companies to provide a platform for wellbeing and inspiration, to support each other and to learn from our collective experience.

Discover Your Bounce Publishing specialises in inspirational stories and business books. We provide mentoring for authors and support from inception of your idea through writing, publishing and cheerleading your book launch. If you have an idea for a book, or a part written manuscript that you want to get over the line, contact Nicky or Sharon on the links below.

Discover Your Bounce For Business provides support for employers who want to improve the staff wellbeing, engagement, culture and performance of their business. We work with CEOs, HR Managers or department heads using practical, easy to implement techniques that create instant change. As we go to print, we have worked with over 2000 employees across the country from a variety of industries and have delivered keynotes at some fantastic international conferences and events.

My Wellbeing supports individuals through individual mentoring and online courses to improve their energy and vision. If your get up and go has got up and gone, get in touch and get bouncing or choose your programme at www.discoveryourbounceacademy.com.

Sharon and Nicky are available to discuss speaking opportunities, wellbeing workshops or private mentoring:

Nicky@discoveryourbounce.com
Sharon@discoveryourbounce.com

You can also find out more on our website:

https://www.discoveryourbounce.com

JOIN US!

You are now part of our community and we would love you to join our Facebook group:

https://www.facebook.com/groups/DiscoverYourBounceCommunity.

THE BOUNCE BACK JOURNEY SERIES

The original Bounce Back Journey was published in February 2020, with no idea of the challenges that were to come. The series continues with The Bounce Back Journey of Women's Health and The Bounce Back Journey of Men's Health, published in November 2020.

COMING IN 2021

The Bounce Back Journey of Gender and Sexuality and The Bounce Back Journey of Parenting are coming soon – register your interest by emailing us at info@discoveryourbounce.com.

SOCIAL PASSION PROJECT

Royalties from these books fund our Social Passion Project, providing mental health awareness training and supporting other important mental health projects. Read more at:

www.discoveryourbounce.com/socialpassionproject.

Printed in Great Britain
by Amazon

61727769R00083